PENNSYLVANIA
Ghost Towns

D1403461

0 11557 03411 0

PENNSYLVANIA
Ghost Towns

UNCOVERING
THE HIDDEN PAST

SUSAN HUTCHISON TASSIN

STACKPOLE
BOOKS

To Jennifer and Joe
The loves of my life

Published by
STACKPOLE BOOKS
5067 Ritter Road
Mechanicsburg, PA 17055
www.stackpolebooks.com

Printed in the United States of America

10 9 8 7 6 5 4 3 2

FIRST EDITION

Design by Beth Oberholtzer
Cover photo by Tom Wenger, www.tomwenger.com
Cover design by Wendy Reynolds

Library of Congress Cataloging-in-Publication Data

Tassin, Susan.
    Pennsylvania ghost towns / Susan Tassin. – 1st ed.
       p.   cm.
    Includes bibliographical references and index.
    ISBN-13: 978-0-8117-3411-0 (pbk.)
    ISBN-10: 0-8117-3411-0 (pbk.)
    1. Ghost towns–Pennsylvania–Guidebooks. 2. Pennsylvania–History, Local. 3. Pennsylvania–Guidebooks. I. Title.

F147.3.T37   2007
974.8–dc22

2007009816

CONTENTS

PREFACE

I have always enjoyed history, especially that of my gorgeous home state, Pennsylvania. But I must admit that I had no idea of the rich history hidden just below the surface throughout much of the commonwealth. This project initially was intended to cover approximately twenty ghost towns but quickly grew to almost fifty. Locals near one site invariably knew of others hidden among the hollows and forests, and finding those led to others.

One of the biggest challenges in writing this book was in the definition of a ghost town. How "gone" must a town be to be included? Some were obvious, with basement foundations, cemeteries, and remnants of roads being all that mark their positions. In other instances, towns by the same name now stand on the site, but the initial settlement was dismantled. Some sites have been turned into tourist attractions, complete with visitors centers and admission fees. In other cases, a few people remain in the original towns, but the towns have ceased to exist in a practical sense. To these remaining residents, I ask your pardon for including your hometown in this book

Each of these towns touched me. Almost every one was special to the people who called it home. Each saw its share of joy and sorrow, laughter and tears, dreams and disappointments. All represented loss as I stood among the ruins.

Some towns had important histories, with plans to house exiled queens or welcome the coming of the Messiah, or as the first site in the world to drill for oil for use as an energy source. Many others were small villages and towns where miners, wildcatters, lumbermen, frontier settlers, and their families lived and worked, but in a way, these were every bit as important. It was these hardworking, brave souls who paved the way for the development of this entire nation. Rural outposts such as these became the backbone on which our nation's economy and culture were built.

My hope is that in writing this book, these sites will survive. Many are in danger of disappearing forever, and a few already have. Perhaps this book will help a few of these towns live on, if only in memory.

A book like this is impossible to write without the help of a lot of people. My editor, Kyle Weaver at Stackpole Books, provided much-appreciated support and encouragement. My parents and children gave me the time and opportunity to take this task on, and I thank them for it. I also thank Mike and Debbie Hutchison and Mary Hutchison for their insightful comments and encouragement. I owe a special thanks to my father, William Hutchison, whose support of this project and tour-guide duties at times were invaluable and provided cherished memories.

The others that helped along the way are many: Lou Bernard, curator extraordinaire from Clinton County Historical Society; Fred Sliter, the "mayor" of Pithole City; Ron and Georgia Blauch; Steve Bottiger; the Pennwriters' Area 5 Writers' Group; the staff at Eastern State Penitentiary; Tom Wenger; and the many historians, curators, docents, enthusiasts, and ghost town seekers who provided me with a surprising number of towns to investigate. If I have failed to mention someone here, it is not from lack of appreciation.

Northwestern Pennsylvania

TEUTONIA

Pennsylvania once provided home to several German communistic societies. One of the largest was Teutonia, in McKean County.

History

The Society of Industry was formed in December 1841, when German immigrants Henry Ginal, William Gilbert, Henry Schweitzer, and William Wernwag purchased 37,000 acres of land in rural McKean County. The founders planned Teutonia as a communal society, in which all property belonged to everyone in the community to be shared. The only exceptions to this were cash money and furniture, which could be owned outright.

Each resident owned equal shares of the town. When joining the society, each male member purchased his share of the community and agreed to do his share of work. Women were considered to be homemakers and were not expected to work outside the home. Children would become society members when they reached adulthood.

Teutonia supported itself mainly through farming and the cattle industry. A few other minor businesses supplemented the town's income.

The town of Teutonia was located near Clermont, south of Smethport. The plans for Teutonia included a Main Street that bisected the town. The northern half of the town contained a church and school, brick plant, repair shop, pottery works, and a planned hotel, which was never completed. Most of the homes in Teutonia were in the northern portion. Along a road named Broadway stood a row of one-and-a-half-story homes. The homes were all exactly alike, in keeping with the communistic beliefs. Each had a single room on the main floor and a small loft for sleeping.

The southern half of the town contained two lodging houses for single residents: one for men, one for women. A general store, communal storage cellar, cabinetmaker's shop, and the community kitchen stood nearby.

Organized religion was a part of life in Teutonia, unlike many other communistic groups. The Society of Industry required that at least 300 shareholders vote to hire a minister. The minister then had to purchase a share of the village, after which he was given a house and board.

The people of Teutonia were industrious, serious-minded people. Besides the agricultural pursuits, several villagers generated income using very different skills. A weaver, watchmaker, carpenter, and baker joined the farmers, potterymakers, brickmakers, and tanners in providing the economic framework of the communistic society.

Initially Teutonia was successful. The townspeople were elated that their economic and social experiment was a success. Soon, however, the laws of economics dealt them a hard blow. Markets for selling Teutonian goods, produce, and meat were distant. Subsequently, the shipping costs began to significantly diminish the profits, and the fortunes of Teutonia suffered.

By 1844, Teutonia was in financial and interpersonal turmoil. The German immigrants who made up the majority of Teutonians grew weary of wearing the bland Teutonian uniform and residing in identical homes. Many residents began to yearn for the opportunity to determine their own destiny and perhaps excel financially on their own. It undoubtedly was difficult for the residents to view the larger, decorated homes of their friends from neighboring villages and compare them to the spartan, charmless cabins in Teutonia.

Henry Ginal, one of the founders of Teutonia, became aware of the unrest in his town. He was asked to reevaluate the documents and constitution of the town and try to come up with some changes that might save it. Ginal promised to do so as soon as he returned from a sudden business trip to Olean. He never returned. The villagers later learned that he had moved to Milwaukee and joined the Freethinker Society. His abandonment was a crushing blow to the community.

Following Ginal's defection, the town crumbled. The homes were abandoned, and the inhabitants dispersed. All subsequently became self-determining, capitalistic Americans.

The Town Today

Unfortunately, nothing remains today of the town of Teutonia. The land it once sat on has been completely bulldozed to make way for new industries.

Directions

The site of Teutonia is located just south of Clermont, off Route 146. A nearby cemetery, east on Route 146, contains the remains of some of the inhabitants and is worth a visit.

PITHOLE CITY

At its peak, the delightfully named Pithole City, in Venango County, would have given any Wild West town a run for its money. It lived a full life in its 500 short days.

History

Pithole City was a marvel of evolution and entropy. The city, located near Titusville in Venango County, was valued at more than $2 million in 1865. In 1878, it was sold to Venango County for $4.37.

How the town came to be named is a somewhat murky issue. Legends of sulfur gases emanating from the pits or holes among the rocks near the local creek apparently led some to believe that the portal to hell was nearby. Others claim that the name simply came from the excavations that took place when drilling for oil. At times, at its zenith, Pithole City probably could have passed as the portal to hell, if the mayhem and odors were any indication.

In September 1865, Pithole City had approximately 15,000 residents. In addition, it had an astonishing fifty-seven hotels. To accommodate the oil workers' needs, it also boasted several brothels and many bars. Briefly, Pithole City had the third-busiest post office in Pennsylvania, as well as its own newspaper. Theaters staged Shakespeare, and pantomime troupes performed at the Athenaeum. Less than a year later, the town was all but deserted.

Pithole City began on the Thomas Holmden farm in Venango County in 1865. Two speculators named Frazier and Faulkner leased the sixty-five acres of farmland in hopes that oil would be found, as much of the oil production in the world at that time was situated in nearby Oil Creek Valley. The men decided to drill on this particular land by using a divining tool made of a witch hazel twig. They were in luck.

The Frazier Well was christened on January 7, 1865. Oil production reached 250 barrels a day. Shortly thereafter, a competing company sank a well just outside the Holmden farm, which also began producing oil at approximately 250 barrels per day.

Almost overnight, thousands of speculators and workers flooded to Pithole City. The land was leased for $3,000 per half-acre plot to speculators, many of whom were Civil War veterans. The land did not belong to the speculator, but rather to the leasors. Subsequently, the resident speculators frequently erected very inexpensive, small buildings in which to live or work. Because many homes and buildings were designed and constructed in a matter of days or weeks, construction was often shoddy and dangerous. All were constructed with wood. No buildings made of stone or brick were built in Pithole City.

One of the more alarming structures in Pithole City was the Astor Hotel, a two-story structure built in its entirety in *one day*. The Astor

Hotel could accommodate sixty guests. Although the townspeople complimented each other throughout the summer on how hastily such structures were put in place, wintertime was a miserable existence, as no insulation and poor construction made for breezy, freezing living conditions. At night, light streamed from the gaps in the wallboards onto the muddy street outside.

The boomtown exploded into existence, but its infrastructure was lacking. Water was scarce in the area and had to be hauled in from distant sites, at great expense. A cup of water cost 10 cents and a pitcher was half a dollar, exorbitant prices in the mid-1800s. There was no sewage system in place, causing the town to absolutely reek. A visitor to Pithole at its peak described it as smelling "like a camp full of soldiers with diarrhea." The town also had no garbage removal system, so dead animals, such as horses and mules, were simply dragged to the edge of town and left to rot. Subsequently, disease was always lurking, and outbreaks of cholera and diphtheria were ever-present threats to residents.

Families and shopkeepers, with no more effective means to eliminate waste, simply opened back doors and pitched out garbage and chamber pot contents. The local gentry would often take off their shoes and socks to cross streets, and then replace them after rinsing their bare feet in buckets provided by local shops.

Besides the human waste, petroleum products posed health threats to residents. Enormous barrels held crude oil within the town, waiting to be carted away. These tanks were open-topped, exposed to weather, leaves, and other pollution. They also presented a constant threat of explosion from fire. Huge signs were posted throughout the town, warning residents that smokers would be lynched. Despite this, the teamsters and drillers defiantly continued to smoke secretly, placing the town's residents at great risk.

Another problem was the poor storage of the pumped oil. The teamsters' horses and mules, used to pull the wagons laden with oil barrels, continually slogged through a slurry consisting of oil and mud. Pithole mules were easy to spot: None had any hair from the neck down. The sludge damaged the capillaries that carried blood to the skin, causing the hair to fall out. At times, the poor beasts were flogged as they tried to drag the tremendously heavy loads through the muddy corduroy tracks to nearby towns. Many dropped dead in their harnesses and were simply dragged to the side of the road. The life expectancy of horses and mules in Pithole City was but a few months. At Pithole's peak, no draft animals were available in a thirty-mile radius around the city. Horses were shipped in from Ohio and New York to work in Pithole.

At first the teamsters were the only feasible way to remove the oil from Pithole and get it to market. Realizing their monopoly, the men quickly began raising their prices. Outcry from the leaseholders did nothing to soften their stance.

In response, the world's first oil pipeline was built in Pithole City and was tested on October 9, 1865. It was developed by Samuel Van Sykle in an attempt to thwart the teamsters' greed. The initial pipeline ran between Pithole and the nearby Miller farm and was quickly followed by several additional pipelines.

The pipelines were effective in transporting the pumped oil and put some 500 teamsters out of work in a matter of weeks. The teamsters retaliated by threatening the oil company officials, sabotaging the pipeline, clashing with guards, and setting the Harley Company oil tanks ablaze. When these tactics didn't work, they quietly lowered the price on their hauling service.

The effect of the price decrease was quite the opposite from what the teamsters had expected. Rather than being grateful for the relief from the high prices, the leaseholders simply argued that it was an acknowledgment that the earlier prices had been intended to gouge the consumers and continued to use the pipelines.

The inhabitants of Pithole were a rather tough lot, mostly adventurous, rowdy men who sought diversions from their daily hard labor. Liquor sales flourished, and there were frequent shootouts and murders in the streets. From all reports, Pithole would have given any Wild West town a run for its money.

Brothels were a source of amusement for the locals and a constant headache for the local police officers. At the Free and Easy brothel, for example, two of the female employees insulted one another, which led to a spirited fistfight, complete with hair pulling and punches. Both were given an overnight stay in jail to calm them-selves. One of the ladies' boyfriends persuaded two of his friends to storm the prison to free his love, but they were unsuccessful and were chased out of town.

The famous boxer Ben Hogan and his prostitute girlfriend, French Kate, lived in Pithole City and ran a popular brothel and saloon. Hogan had nicknamed himself "the wickedest man in the world," although his reasons for doing so are unclear. His past is murky and undocumented, but it appears that he had a history of work in enter-tainment, including boxing and gymnastics exhibitions.

Upon moving to Pithole City in February 1866, Hogan began earning a living entertaining crowds with violent boxing matches or gymnastics. His matches often ended with near riots breaking out between the groups of rival fans.

French Kate became a madame in Pithole, running a successful brothel. Hogan served as her pimp and agent, procuring young women to work in the establishment. Kate's girls often rode naked on horse-back through Pithole on Sunday mornings to advertise their services.

French Kate was a rough character. Although never proven, Kate was rumored to have been involved in the plot to assassinate President Lincoln. She supposedly had some interaction with John Wilkes Booth, who briefly speculated in oil in the valley before pursuing his dream of being an actor as well as his interest in politics. Booth later assassinated President Lincoln.

Ben Hogan was enterprising in his quest to find new young pros-titutes for Kate. One technique was to place ads in newspapers in upstate New York, seeking nannies for respectable families in Pithole. When the unsuspecting girls arrived, they were pressed into service in French Kate's brothel.

One such young lady, Rebecca, applied for the job and arrived in town. Upon realizing that her employers were not a family in need of a nanny, but expected her to prostitute herself, she refused. The seventeen-year-old was imprisoned on the second floor of the brothel and starved in an attempt to force her to submit. She somehow man-aged to write a letter to her mother and have it smuggled from the building. The letter was found, unstamped, in the road and was dropped into the mail. Remarkably, the letter was delivered to the girl's mother, who raced to Pithole City to save her daughter.

The girl's hysterical mother begged French Kate and Ben Hogan to release her daughter, but the two denied any knowledge of her existence or whereabouts. In desperation, the mother turned to the local pastor to intervene. Reverend Steadman, with three armed friends, visited Ben Hogan.

At first Hogan denied the girl's existence, but when the four men drew pistols and pointed them at his head, he suddenly regained his memory. He apologized for his brief memory slip and ordered the girl's release to her mother.

In 1866, oil production began to slow dramatically as the wells dried up. In addition, several devastating fires sealed the fate of the town as a dying entity. The first fire occurred on August 2, 1865, at the Grant Well. The well had at first appeared dry, but then suddenly began pumping oil. A crowd of about 100 gathered to watch the oil flow. Not expecting such an increase in output, the owners did not have provisions to catch the oil in place, and it ran unencumbered across the ground, into the rutted road, and to the creek.

An explosion, probably caused by the heat generated by the pumping mechanism, ripped through the celebrating crowd, seriously injuring twenty, one of whom later died of his wounds. The fire consumed an area spanning an acre in a matter of moments, with flames leaping more than 100 feet in the air.

More fires were to follow. The flimsy wooden structures that composed the town were kindling in front of oil-rich flames. The scarcity of water made firefighting difficult at best. The devastation from the fires, combined with the dwindling oil flow from the wells, sealed the fate of Pithole City. Most remaining residents, discouraged, simply abandoned their leases.

The Town Today

Today little remains of Pithole City. A small visitors center onsite hosts lectures and occasional tours of the site. (Lantern tours in October are very popular; call ahead and arrive early.) The "mayor" of Pithole City, Fred Sliter, who is knowledgeable about the site and the general area, currently runs the visitors center. A detailed diorama of the town at its height of activity makes the visitors center worth visiting, and you can view a videotaped history of the area. A gift shop and restrooms are available. The museum's hours are irregular; it is recommended that you check the hours online or call ahead if you plan to visit. There is a nominal admission fee.

Indentations where cellars were sunken and the outlines of roads are still visible to visitors. Street signs mark the roads clearly, and detailed signs throughout the site show the locations of many of the original buildings. It is illegal to treasure hunt here; leave your metal detector at home. Benches placed throughout the site allow you to sit and imagine the rich history of the town. A picnic pavilion with barbecue pits is also available.

Stories of encounters with ghosts are plentiful at Pithole City today. Many visitors report seeing French Kate, accompanied by a sudden drop in temperature. Some say that they have seen Ben Hogan. Though these reports are intriguing, a story told by the curator of the site gives one pause.

The curator of Pithole City, Fred Sliter, has never personally experienced any paranormal phenomena. Many visitors tell him about the ghosts they have seen on the site, and he listens politely. But one such report haunted him, so to speak.

In the early 1990s, an elderly couple was visiting Pithole City from Ohio. Fred was working on the property and sat down to rest on one of the benches. The couple joined him and asked whether any reenactments were currently happening on the property. Fred informed them that Pithole City did not do reenactments. The two looked a bit confused and told Fred that they had just spoken to a man in period dress at the corner of Holmden and First Streets. The man introduced himself as Alexander Payne and told them that he was surprised at the condition of the town. He said that he had formerly worked in Pithole.

Fred was unfamiliar with the name. After returning to the visitors center, and noting only his and the couple's cars in the parking lot, he researched the name of Alexander Payne. No such person had ever lived in Pithole.

Several years later, Fred and other museum employees were working on a nearby site and came across a cemetery. Fred searched and found a grave for a man named Alexander Payne, who lived near the cemetery's site and commuted to work in Pithole City each day. Was he visiting the town in which he had worked for some time?

Directions

Follow Route 27 east from Titusville, then take Route 227. Follow signs for the turnoff to Pithole, which is between Pleasantville and Plumer.

STRAIGHT

Located in Elk County near the now-submerged ghost lumber town of Instanter lies the watery grave of Straight, Pennsylvania.

History

Quinn and Company, along with Henry, Bayard, and Company, founded Straight in a location along the Clarion River around 1895. A lumbermill was located where the Straight Creek flowed into the river from the east.

The company store and office were built first, with lumber brought from nearby Quinnwood. The store was large: 60 feet wide by 150 feet long, in a two-story frame. A hand-propelled elevator joined the two floors. The employees purchased items in the store on credit, which was weighed against their pay at the end of the month. The store's manager was widely regarded as a reasonable man. In times of difficulty, debts were forgiven. If a worker couldn't work because of illness, the store provided food to carry the sick man through. If a worker's wife was spending too much money, the store notified the worker, and the woman's shopping was limited.

Other buildings in town included a barbershop and a billiard hall. On the second floor of the billiard hall building, a large room was used for square dancing on weekend evenings. Occasionally a movie was shown on a sheet on the wall. The town also had a Catholic church, built in 1904. Before the church's construction, worshippers used a barn for their services.

Initially kerosene lamps illuminated the inside of the lumbermill. But because of the high risk of fire, which was an ever-present threat in the lumber industry, a generator began providing the electricity to light the mill, the lumberyard, and even the company store in 1903.

Besides the lumbermill, Quinn and Company also built a chemical plant in town. Soon two other companies founded chemical plants nearby. The work attracted Italian immigrant workers, who lived in a shanty town on the outskirts of Straight. The men who actually cut the lumber and stripped the bark in Straight consisted of Swedish-descent Americans and some French workers. The men who were employed to cut the cordwood tended to be Swedish, Austrian, Polish, and Italian.

The workers' houses were essentially identical. All had two stories, with a kitchen, living area, and two bedrooms on the first floor and four bedrooms on the second floor. There was no sewer system, so all houses had outhouses.

The forest camps for the lumbermen, who were called wood hicks, tended to be rough places, in terms of standard of living. The men were expected to provide their own straw- or cornhusk-stuffed mattresses and cooking implements. Twice a week, the supply car made its trip to the camps. The train conductor dropped off the current order of groceries and took the supply order for the next trip. The supply car typically brought such items as beef, prepared hogs, salt pork, potatoes, beans, oatmeal and cornmeal, spices such as salt and pepper, eggs, milk, and kerosene for light. In addition, supplies for the horses and mules were provided. The Italian workers complained bitterly about the lack of bread, prompting the Quinn company to build a bakery in town, hire an Italian baker, and supply the camps with Italian bread.

Unlike many lumber camps, in which alcohol was strictly forbidden, it flowed freely in Straight. Beer and whiskey were shipped in from St. Mary's weekly, and the wood hicks often rolled entire kegs to their camps to enjoy. Needless to say, frequent raucous fights broke out in the camps among the various ethnic groups.

The town had a rather unusual interest in aesthetics that many other lumber towns did not share. Parts of town included lovely painted homes, with yards complete with shade and fruit trees. The company even allowed virgin hemlock forest to surround the town, shielding the ugly clear-cutting from view, until the very end of the supply was reached. These trees were the last to be cut in 1909. At that time, the lumbermill was closed and dismantled, and its building materials were shipped elsewhere.

The chemical plants continued to operate for some time after the mill closed, shipping in hardwood from other areas of the state. Eventually they too closed, around 1923. The town rapidly emptied as workers moved on to other employment.

The Town Today

Like the nearby town of Instanter, Straight is deep underwater. In 1948, the U.S. government built the East Branch Flood Control Dam, flooding the entire valley in which Straight stood.

Straight briefly emerged from its watery tomb in 1991 during a drought. At that time, little remained to suggest that a busy lumber town had once stood on the site.

BETULA

Betula is located in McKean County in a pretty area of the state. Several company homes still stand, with current families living within.

History

Betula was founded sometime around 1910. The town grew rapidly when the Betula Stave Company, a barrelmaking business, was built. Local lumbermills provided wood to the barrel factory. With 3,500 residents, the town had a hotel, jail, billiard lounge, barbershop, lovely theater, and livery stables. A taxicab, a rare luxury, was available to convey residents between Betula, Norwich, and Colgrove.

The billiard lounge did not supply alcohol to its customers, nor did any other businesses in Betula. The period of time in which Betula flourished was during the time of Prohibition in America. To circumvent these restrictions, some of the workers built stills out in the woods to supply their liquor. The partying was kept relatively quiet, however, as the men ran the risk of losing their jobs if they were caught imbibing. Some made the trip to the nearby town of Clermont, which had a much more liberal view of alcohol consumption.

As with all lumber towns, it was the hardworking men who made the town successful. The men who cut the lumber for the barrel company were called wood hicks. They numbered in the thousands around Betula and lived in the woods and mountains in huts and tents. They came down out of the woods to town once a month, on payday. They stayed in town until they had partied to their hearts' and wallets' content, and then returned to the woods empty-handed. These were rugged men who worked hard and bathed infrequently. They, not surprisingly, were typically unmarried and lived alone or in small groups in rustic huts and shanty towns around Betula.

By 1922, the forests surrounding Betula had been stripped bare for miles around, which was the lament of many a logging town. The barrel factory closed, as did the lumbermills. Betula quickly died out, having no other significant businesses to sustain it. Many of the local houses and other buildings were dismantled, and the materials were taken elsewhere to be used again in construction.

The Town Today

A few original homes still stand in Betula, with families living in them today. Little remains to remind visitors of the busy little town that once claimed to have "everything a larger city had, only smaller." Remains of the barrel mill and lumbermill, including foundations, are reportedly located just north of the main road in Betula.

Directions

From Smethport, take Route 46 south for 12.5 miles. The right-hand turn to Betula is marked by a road sign. Follow the Betula Road, noting the older homes on either side. These were the original company houses. A dirt road leading from the right reportedly leads to the foundations of the stave factory and possibly the lumbermills.

PETROLEUM CENTER

Petroleum Center, in Venango County, played an important role in the history of Pennsylvania. It also played a critical role in the development of petroleum's use as a fuel, which changed the world.

History

Petroleum Center is approximately midway between Titusville and Oil City, which became oil centers around 1859. Petroleum Center began to pump oil in 1861 and reached its peak in 1869. In 1864, the Central Petroleum Company purchased the G. W. McClintock farm and formed a town. The company leased land to speculators, with the stipulation that the company would own half of any oil that was found. They also added that any building could be torn down on thirty days' notice to put in a new well. Because of this, almost all homes and businesses were made of inexpensive materials, and construction practice was shoddy at best.

Living space in Petroleum Center was at a premium. Visitors planning a trip to the town were cautioned to pack lightly. Rooms and beds were difficult to come by, and storage for personal items was almost nonexistent. Visitors often shared beds with a stranger, if they were lucky enough to get one at all.

At its most prolific, the town boasted 5,000 residents. Oil and entertainment were considered to be the major industries of the town. The Opera House was an important cultural landmark in Petroleum Center. One of its more impressive acts was that of Billy Moorhead, entitled "The Only Man in the Country Who Can Write Up and Down with Both Hands at the Same Time."

Besides the Opera House, Petroleum Center was home to a bank, three churches, twelve dry-goods stores, several hotels, brokerage offices, livery stables, gambling houses, saloons, and brothels. The town was entirely company-owned, so there was no municipal government and no appreciable law enforcement, other than the county sheriff. There was no public sanitation service or public works of any kind. Subsequently, it was a rather odoriferous, dirty place for the most part. Raw sewage mixed with garbage that townspeople flung from their doorways.

One of the more prominent and wealthy citizens of Petroleum Center was George H. Bissel, who owned the local bank. Bissel was a pivotal person in world history, as he was the first person to realize the illuminative capabilities of petroleum. His 1853 discovery created an entirely new form of fuel for light and heat in the world, which continues to be used today. Bissel began the world's first petroleum company in 1854, the Pennsylvania Rock Oil Company.

The term "wildcatter" was coined in Petroleum Center. A speculator in a neighboring valley shot a wildcat on his lease, stuffed it, and placed it atop his oil derrick. Subsequent visitors to the area referred to the area as Wildcat Hollow and called the local citizens, who risked drilling for oil in unproven territory, wildcatters.

Crime was a significant problem in Petroleum Center. That the town had no police force certainly was of some comfort to the criminals who called Petroleum Center home. Described in the local paper as a town of "pure, unadulterated wickedness," Petroleum Center struggled with how to contain the criminal element with limited resources in a company town. With little law enforcement, lawbreakers faced no censure for their acts.

The crime of sandbagging was rampant. Thugs would fill bags with sand, approach pedestrians from behind, strike them, and steal their belongings. Reports of crime were so common that when a waitress was shot in Tom Quirk's saloon, so much other mayhem claimed space in the local paper that the shooting was barely mentioned.

The livery stables in town did a swift business in providing horses and mules to teamsters, the men who drove the wagons full of oil barrels from the town. The local oil teamsters were known to many as dirty fighters. They had a well-earned reputation for biting off noses, lips, and ears during brawls. Prospecting forty-niners, passing through the area panning for gold, were horrified by the brutality of the oil teamsters during the requisite barroom fights. The forty-niners preferred to cleanly shoot their opponents.

As oil production declined, so too did the town. Workers and their families moved on to other employment in areas throughout the Northeast.

The Town Today

Over the last several decades, the state government claimed eminent domain over Petroleum Center, and the families who remained left the area. The sad loss of their homes has had the positive impact of providing the world with the ability to visit an important site in the quest for energy sources. The site is now part of the 7,000-acre Oil Creek State Park, with camping, hiking, fishing, cross-country skiing, and railroad rides.

Today little remains of Petroleum Center as it was. Most structures from the peak of oil production were constructed poorly from degradable products such as wood. A concrete step near the iron bridge remains as one of the few true artifacts of the bygone era. It was the original step of the George H. Bissel and Company Bank.

A well-marked historical walking path begins at the ranger station. The forty-five-minute walk is easy, handicapped-accessible, and incorporates highly informative markers telling the history and human-interest stories from the period when the town provided a significant portion of the world's petroleum. The train station, located along the walk, houses some interesting photos and a detailed diorama of the town. It is staffed by a knowledgeable curator.

Oil Creek State Park is free of charge and is open year-round. The train station is also free but is open only from June through October. Bicycle rentals are available at the house across from the ranger station. Picnic tables are plentiful, and there are many hiking trails through the park.

The town's cemetery is located on a trail off SR 1009, as you exit the area to drive to Titusville. It is clearly marked by a sign. You can get a key to open the trail gate from the ranger station or park and take the short hike up the trail to the cemetery. There are surprisingly few graves here. As you return on the trail to your vehicle, look to your left and peer through the woods. A few dozen yards away from the main cemetery is the McClintock family plot, surrounded by a short concrete fence. The gravestones are in some disrepair.

Directions

Petroleum Center is located in Oil Creek State Park, just off Route 8, about 3 miles north of Oil City. It is a few miles west of Pithole City, another ghost town highlighted in this book.

PEALE

Peale existed from 1883 to 1912 and lies in a beautiful stretch of Clearfield County near Snow Shoe.

History

The coal-mining town of Peale was named after Sen. S. R. Peale of Lock Haven. It was a rather large company town, with some 300 buildings. At its height, 2,500 people called Peale home.

The Clearfield Bituminous Coal Company or the Beech Creek Railroad owned every structure in Peale and employed all working residents. The workers' houses were all similar—two-story frame buildings painted red. Each had three rooms on the ground floor and two or three rooms on the second floor. The coal company charged rent varying from $4.25 to $6.75. Rent included running water, which was provided from a reservoir behind the town.

Many of the town's residents were Swedish. Others were of Scottish descent. One Scotswoman, Martha Renfrew, lies at rest under the last standing gravestone in the Oakwood Cemetery. She and her husband sailed to America in 1870. After the death of her husband in 1877, Martha moved to Peale, where she lived until her death in May 1886. Poignantly, her gravestone simply states, "I was."

The coal company owned the store in town, which provided almost every imaginable item to the residents. The only item that was not sold in the store was alcohol, which the company discouraged. Other buildings included a large town hall that served as a community meeting place and also housed a theater. Peale also had an Episcopal church. All other denominations were not so fortunate, however, and conducted their services in the town hall. The town's sidewalks were made of wooden boardwalks, which provided pedestrians with a relatively mud-free stroll through town.

The manager of Peale's mining operations was George Platt. He was described as a fair man, and most men working in the town were content with their lot in life. In 1880, miners earned $11.50 a week for their services, and drivers in the mines $10 a week. In 1902, railroad laborers made 13 cents an hour, and railroad foremen 55 cents an hour.

The coal seam below the town proved to be largely unprofitable. Instead, the Peale workers had to hike three miles to Grassflat to mine there. The miners soon became tired of the long commute each morning and evening, especially in poor weather. One by one, they moved their families to Grassflat. The coal company closed up operations in Peale in 1912, although some hardy residents remained until the 1940s.

The Town Today

Some foundations can still be found in Peale. They are located near some cabins in the area. The former residents of Peale continue to gather and communicate, and they work hard to keep the memory of their beloved town alive.

Directions

From Clearfield, Pennsylvania, take Route 322 east. Merge onto Route 879, and then turn onto Route 80 east. Take Exit 133 toward Kylertown/Philipsburg. Turn left onto Route 53. Turn right onto

Johnsons Road, which becomes SR 2039. Peale Road is straight ahead. Once you are on Peale Road, the town of Peale is a little over 1.5 miles ahead.

NORWICH

A huge department store and chauffered Cadillac in a rural lumber town? Norwich, in McKean County, proved to be a cut above others.

History

Norwich was founded in 1910, when the Goodyear Lumber Company built a large sawmill on Potato Creek. The mill consisted of the main building, which housed two enormous band saws; a planing mill; and a boiler house. It employed more than 100 men, who lived in Norwich or the surrounding woods.

Of the 5,000 residents of Norwich, 4,000 were wood hicks, who cut wood for the mill and the Keystone Chemical Plant. They were a rather rough bunch who lived in huts and shanties in the woods around the town. They often converged in town once a month to pick up their paychecks. They celebrated and spent their wages until they were broke, and then returned to the woods.

The homes in Norwich were a bit more comfortable than those in many other logging towns. The Goodyear Company had built a water plant to pump spring water into every home in town. Each house also had its own bathroom, a sewer system, and access to natural gas for warmth and light.

Norwich was a busy town, with a kindling factory, a hotel, shops, Protestant and Catholic churches, a movie theater, and its own fire department. A department store, owned by Charles Hull, was the most successful business in town. The store was gigantic and contained goods to provide for the needs and whims of every inhabitant in Norwich and its neighboring towns. Hull devised a unique system to increase business and pamper his lady customers. He provided two chauffered Cadillac limousines to pick up the local ladies at their homes, wait while they shopped, and then return them to their homes with their packages. Hull's store was so popular that it put every other shop in Norwich out of business.

While the mill was in service, the Goodyear Company cleared 26,000 acres of timber. This translated into almost 400 million board feet of lumber produced, along with an additional 90 million feet of hardwood to be turned into staves at nearby Betula's Stave Company. But by 1920, the area's timber reserves were depleted. The mill shut down and was dismantled and taken to Clarion County, where it was reassembled and put back into service. The railroad soon stopped running to Norwich, after which the town rapidly emptied. Most houses were demolished, but some were broken down and moved to Austin or other nearby towns.

The Town Today

It is difficult to imagine the busy town of Norwich when looking at it today. Most of the key buildings are gone, although five of the company houses still are homes to local residents.

Directions

From U.S. Route 6, take Route 46 south for 11.2 miles. Just past the sign for Betula lies the location of Norwich. As the road begins to rise, you will pass the site of the Norwich Catholic Church. There is a pulloff parking area. To the right of Route 46 was Hull's department store.

LOLETA

Today Loleta is a beautiful recreation area in Elk County. It seems a fitting, restful end to a once busy Pennsylvania lumber town.

History

Loleta was founded in 1898 by the Amsler and Campbell Company, which built a sawmill and town on the site. By 1899, the first lumber was being cut, and the town rapidly developed into a busy community.

Early on, besides the lumbermill, Loleta also had a broom-handle factory, shingle mill, two-room schoolhouse, livery stable, company store, blacksmith shop, post office, two boardinghouses, and almost thirty homes. By late 1900, with the addition of a night shift at the mill, the town grew to more than a hundred homes.

The Loleta company store was considered to be the heart of the community. It sold everything from basic groceries to shoes and boots, hardware, and paper products. Ladies bought fabric and other sewing supplies at the store, as well as medicines and penny candy. The Loleta store also served as the community's bank. Like many other company stores, it did most purchases on credit, which were then paid off on payday.

This system of banking and credit was common in company towns. Though it was a convenient way to do business, it had the secondary effects of discouraging the workers from controlling their expenses or bargain shopping when possible, as no commerce competition was permitted, and it kept them poor enough that they were unable to leave the town.

Loleta had no formal churches. Instead, traveling ministers visited and held services in a room above the company store. The Sundays alternated between a Methodist service and a Presbyterian service.

Fire was a constant threat to any lumber town. Loleta barely survived a devastating forest fire in 1902. Out of concern about fires, smoking was banned in the sawmill. The lumbermen chewed tobacco while at work, although smoking was permitted within the store. The store was famous for carrying many different brands and flavors of tobacco. Visitors from other nearby towns frequently walked the distance to Loleta to stock up on tobacco.

On any given evening, the store was filled with tired workers, smoking pipes, talking politics and gossip, and playing checkers. The store didn't have its own checkerboard, so someone made a board from a piece of wood with squares drawn in chalk. Pink and white mint candies served as the checkers.

The houses in Loleta had no running water or sewer system. Instead, outhouses served as bathrooms, and housewives lugged heavy buckets of water from the local wells. Residents bathed in washtubs infrequently, since all water had to be carried some distance from the town well. Some creative men in town rigged up a hot and cold running shower in a makeshift bathhouse that was available for use only by those who had helped build it. Others eyed it enviously but did not use it for fear of reprisal.

Loleta had just two telephones, both located in the company offices. One was an outside Bell telephone, which provided the only link with the outside world. The other was a local phone, used mainly to summon the local doctor.

There were no taverns in Loleta, so the young men of the town often rented horses at the livery stable and made their way to the town of Marienville, six miles away. There they would party and spend their hard-earned money, knowing that even if they fell asleep on the horse on the return trip, the animal would find its way home.

Another outing for the working men of Loleta was to board the train to nearby Sheffield. After drinking all evening, many of them regularly ended up sleeping it off in the Sheffield jail. As a matter of course, every Sunday afternoon the men were collected and put into a baggage car to sober up on the trip back to Loleta. The conductor and brakeman ran the same route each weekend and personally made sure that each man made it home safely.

The main lumber office in Williamsport had appointed a division superintendent to supervise many of the mill operations. Although the man was a nice enough fellow, he was universally resented in Loleta. He was viewed not only as an outsider, but also as a spy for the company. The workers at Loleta were generally a cohesive bunch and often covered for each other, but the presence of the division superintendent created an atmosphere of paranoia and insecurity in the community. He always arrived unannounced, and his reports were secret, never viewed by anyone in town. The only way the workers knew what the man's concerns were was when a letter came from Williamsport ordering some change in behavior or work technique.

The division superintendent had a habit of leaning against a supporting post in the mill as he watched the men work. Inexplicably, this post became thickly coated with axle grease. After one ruined suit, the man learned to stand up straight while he made his observations. After several other practical jokes were played on the man, he made it a practice to visit the mill only when accompanied by the mill manager.

The Loleta lumbermill sawed almost 35 million board feet in the year 1906, but by 1907, the forests were becoming depleted, and Loleta's mill cut back to one shift per day. By 1910, the forests had been cleared. The lumbermill completely closed in February 1913. The town was dismantled, and its inhabitants moved away.

The Town Today

Loleta is now a recreation area within the Allegheny National Forest. The Loleta Recreation Area has swimming areas and beaches, public bathrooms with hot showers, hiking trails, thirty-eight campsites, and a picnic area. The area has excellent trout fishing in Millstone Creek.

In the 1930s during the Depression, the Civilian Conservation Corps set up a camp at Loleta, where they built a dam and reconstructed the old millpond. This dam now serves as a boundary to the swimming hole in the state park. The CCC also built the present-day bathhouse on the site.

Directions

Loleta is located 6 miles south of Marienville, in Elk County. From Route 66 in Marienville, drive south on Loleta Road.

INSTANTER

Visiting the former Elk County town of Instanter today is a bit challenging, unless you have scuba gear and flippers.

History

Following the completion in 1889 of the Johnsonburg and Clermont Railroad through the wilds of Elk County, the sawmill town of Instanter was born. Like many lumber towns, it exploded into existence, with mills, homes, roads, stores, churches, and hotels built seemingly overnight.

The town was actually named New Instanter at first, although in later years New was dropped from the name. There had been a village named Instanter on the site of the current hamlet of Clermont. It had been a burgeoning community of many log homes, a school, a church, and the offices of the Holland Land Company. But with the beginning of the War of 1812, the people of the original Instanter deserted it, fearful that a British victory in the war would bring reprisals to the remote, unprotected village. The buildings were torn down, and the original Instanter was no more.

The town of New Instanter was located at the intersection of Seven Mile Creek and Instanter Run. J. B. Hoyt Jr. and Norman Schultz chose the site for a tannery because of the abundance of water and endless hemlock forests, both critical for the leather-tanning process. Wealthy businessman Henry Schimmelfeng also built a large sawmill in New Instanter. Besides providing lumber for building purposes, the mill stripped the hemlock bark and sold it to the local tannery.

The tannery was housed in a building 250 feet long. Two storage buildings were adjacent, each of which were 300 feet long. The drying house was a two-story structure and was 400 feet long. In addition, the Tannery Company provided about thirty houses for the workers and several more substantial homes for the management of the tannery.

Schimmelfeng built a general store and post office, which was manned by his son, Charles Schimmelfeng. With the opening of the post office, the name of New Instanter was officially changed to Instanter.

Schimmelfeng was a philanthropist as well as a successful businessman. Hailing from Warren, Pennsylvania, at one point he learned that the Warren Hospital was in dire need of renovation and offered to donate $5,000 to the project if ten other men would do the same. Other donors were quickly found, and the renovations and expansion were completed.

A frequent occurrence in lumber towns, the sawmill burned in March 1897. With a large stretch of timber still in the mountains uncut, Schimmelfeng realized that some profit had yet to be reaped from the forests surrounding Instanter. He decided to rebuild quickly. He wanted a mill that was even larger than the first, but as profits were critical, it needed to be erected immediately. He hired a man named William Collum as contractor for the job, telling him that if he could have the mill completed within three months, an incredibly short time, he would receive a bonus of $200. Collum rallied to the task, completed the work on time, and received his bonus. He reportedly delayed cashing the check for some time, instead carrying it around and waving it in the air around town, showing off his windfall to his friends and neighbors. In the late 1800s, $200 was a significant amount of money.

The newly built mill had an output capacity of 75,000 board feet of lumber each day. It also had the capability of turning out broom handles, stove wood, and wooden lath, thus increasing the profitability of the mill. Schimmelfeng was very pleased with his new income opportunities.

But inevitably the forests around Instanter were emptied of trees, and by 1902 a stark landscape was left in their place. Subsequently, the lumber company folded, and the mill was shut down. It was sold, broken down, and moved to Cameron, Pennsylvania, where it was rebuilt. Schimmelfeng moved from his gorgeous mansion on a hill overlooking Instanter and returned to the Warren area. The large home was then sold to Daniel Hogan in 1903.

Hogan was a cut-stone contractor. An industrious man, he built a small tramway from Instanter to his quarry at the top of the hill and moved the rocks along it. He was very successful in his venture and continued to provide cut stone for the foundations of many homes and businesses in the area. He eventually became ill and closed his business. He sold the mansion, finding the upkeep too much to manage in his weakened state. The Schimmelfeng Mansion was sold in 1914 to the St. John's Episcopal Mission Chapel, which had previously held its services in the local school building.

The mansion-turned-chapel was briefly used as an emergency hospital in 1918, when an influenza outbreak threatened the town. More than 100 townspeople became desperately ill and were cared for in the chapel. A doctor visited daily, accompanied by a nurse and volunteers from the local area. The patients were not charged for their care, as public donations covered the cost. It is notable that only two patients lost their lives during this epidemic that killed so many. It stands as a testament to the loving care provided by the medical staff and volunteers that more victims did not succumb to the sickness.

Life in Instanter was generally peaceful and quaint. The townspeople took great pride in their local baseball team, which played against teams from other towns around the area. On clear summer evenings, the music of the local cornet band filled the air. Further proof of Instanter's interest in culture and art, a literary society was formed, with forty-five members who met weekly. Young women in the town also formed a Junior Guild and a secret society, the Ancient Order of Gobblers. These groups hosted many social events, and membership was much sought after.

Howe's Hotel was the site of many dances and parties, attracting young people from neighboring towns. A sample menu from the hotel for Christmas Day 1910 included the following for the grand sum of 40 cents: celery and olives, cream of chicken soup, roast goose, stewed chicken and dumplings, roast turkey with cranberry sauce, spare ribs with brown gravy, mashed potatoes, boiled rice, applesauce, stewed tomatoes, Christmas plum pudding, grape jelly, mince pie, vanilla ice cream, delicate cake, fruit, confections, and coffee.

In 1926, the Elk Tanning Company announced that the tannery in Instanter would close its doors a few days before Christmas. The cost of importing the bark for the tanning process had simply become prohibitive. This was a devastating blow to the economy of Instanter. The tannery's brick smokestack was dynamited, creating a useless heap of a quarter million bricks. Deprived of one of its last industries, the town became largely deserted.

In 1928, some of the land was purchased by Mrs. James K. Gardner, who donated it to the YMCA of Ridgway for a youth camp. A swimming pool, tennis courts, and baseball fields were built and were enjoyed by many children attending camp. The use of the camp was discontinued in 1934, however, because of the Depression.

In 1948, the U.S. government acquired the land in the Instanter area. It constructed the nearby East Branch Flood Control Dam, which placed the town site completely underwater.

The Town Today

To visit Instanter today, you need to float above it in a boat. But the memories of this town are kept alive by its former residents at annual reunions and picnics, as well as by local historians.

GARDEAU

Is there lost treasure near this town site in McKean County?

History

Gardeau (pronounced Gar-DOO) was once a productive lumber town, located at the far southern edge of McKean County. A sawmill, of which Col. Noah Parker was part owner, was built in 1891. It burned in 1893, was rebuilt, and burned again in 1897. Parker presided over the town and the lumbermill.

The sawmill provided employment for many hardworking men in the area. The workers lived in small houses, some of which are used today as hunting camps. Colonel Parker's presence in Gardeau makes for a fascinating tale. He was commissioned by a Captain Blackbeard (not the famous Blackbeard whose proper name was Edward Teach). This Blackbeard was a British seaman hired in 1811 to raise a Spanish galleon in the Caribbean, on which there was a $1.5 million fortune in silver bars. The ship had gone down in a hurricane in the autumn of 1680. As the ship was in shallow water, Blackbeard, renowned as an expert at marine salvage, had no difficulty raising it. He then surrounded the damaged ship with pontoons and prepared to tow his prize to port.

As England was at war with France at the time of the salvage, Blackbeard determined that it would be unsafe to take the galleon to any port in Great Britain. Instead, as an ocean storm forced a quick decision, Blackbeard towed the galleon to Baltimore. He then made arrangements to have a warship tow the ship to England.

One evening before the warship was employed, Blackbeard was relaxing in a Baltimore pub. He met a privateer named Peter Abelhard Karthaus, of the ship *Comet*. Karthaus told an appalled Blackbeard that he had heard of an Englishman bringing a Spanish galleon and $1.5 million to Baltimore.

Blackbeard was forced into action. Privateers posed a more formidable threat than French warships. He decided to take the fortune to safety in Canada, about 400 miles north. Most of the route would take Blackbeard through sparsely populated forest, which would provide some cover for his purpose.

The captain decided to follow the Susquehanna River to Williamsport, and from there continue up the Sinnemahoning River until he reached what is now Emporium, Pennsylvania. He would then have to portage twenty-three miles over Keating Summit to the Allegheny River. From the Allegheny River, he could easily make it to Lake Erie, which was controlled by the British. From there, his treasure would be safe.

He loaded the silver into wagons with false bottoms and covered them with straw. Along with guards with loyalties to Britain, he began his journey.

But Blackbeard had underestimated the difficulty of his route. Once he reached Lycoming County, several capsizing rafts dumped his oxen and wagons into the freezing river.

During his trip, war broke out between Great Britain and America, which made his position even more precarious. He began to suspect that some of his guards had loyalties to America and they might betray him. On hearing that Lake Erie was no longer secure from the Americans, he decided to complete the twenty-three-mile portage and simply bury his treasure.

Just south of Keating Summit, Blackbeard buried his enormous treasure near a salt lick for safekeeping. He believed that the impenetrable wilderness would help protect it, and he could return for it after England successfully defeated the Americans.

Blackbeard returned to England and informed his superiors of his actions. He arranged to have Col. Noah Parker travel to the site and safeguard it. Parker did an excellent job, keeping the Americans from finding the treasure, but also delaying Blackbeard from reclaiming it. When letters from Blackbeard arrived in Gardeau, asking the status of the treasure, Parker always responded that he had not yet found it. Whether Parker was being truthful is a subject of much speculation. Within a few years, Blackbeard had died, and the treasure was forgotten by most.

Parker always denied having the treasure to locals who asked. Tales of Parker having bouts of "sudden affluence" over the years were rampant, but no proof exists that he ever found or spent the treasure. He died without ever divulging the location of the treasure.

Colonel Parker opened one of the first spas in northern Pennsylvania and enjoyed regaling guests with tales of the treasure. Assuming that he did not take it, no one has ever found the treasure, which is now estimated to be worth approximately $5 million.

The Town Today

Gardeau is mostly populated with hunting camps. An old church remains, as do several obvious foundations from the era of the lumber center. One of the most intriguing facets of the village is the mausoleum of Colonel Parker, which sits slightly elevated to overlook the area. The tomb is obvious and clearly marked. Building foundations are scattered nearby. The large open area across the road from Parker's tomb was reportedly the site of the sawmill.

Directions

From Emporium, Cameron County, take Route 155 north to Sizerville. In Sizerville, veer left onto Gardeau Road, which will take you directly to the ghost town, just over the McKean County line. Look for Col. Noah Parker's tomb on your left.

CLERMONT

The few remaining residents of Clermont, in McKean County, may take umbrage at being named inhabitants of a ghost town, but it's almost impossible to picture an opera house in this area now consisting largely of hunting cabins.

History

Clermont began as a coal-mining town, with the Buffalo Coal Company investing in several mines around the area. The Buffalo Coal Mine was opened in the Clermont area in 1874 and quickly became the most profitable mine in the area. The Gum Boot Mine was opened a short distance away in 1879 and also became successful. The two mines provided the foundation of employment and population for the area.

But by 1883 fortunes had turned, and the mines were struggling with local competition from other mining companies. By the summer of 1885, the mines were closed. The loss of the mines was devastating for the economy of Clermont, but the industrious Pennsylvanians soon found another way to exploit the natural resources of the area. They began mining the clay from the Gum Boot Mine for use in a new endeavor. In 1901, Clermont became the home of the Clermont Tile Company. The name of this factory changed several times, becoming the Clermont Sewer Pipe Company and later the Kaul Clay Company. The factory took the clay mined nearby, treated it, fired it in a kiln, and sold the final products as tiles for walls, flues, and foundations.

During its heyday, the town of Clermont was known as a rather wild place. Unlike many company towns, alcohol could be found in some proliferation in Clermont. The town had a pool hall and several bars, which tended to add to the rough-and-tumble reputation of the town. At times, workers from neighboring towns made their way to Clermont to enjoy the libations. There were frequent brawls and small riots, often based on ethnicity. The Italian workers were viewed with great suspicion by many of the other workers, which may have been related to the activities in the area of the criminal Black Hand organization, a precursor to the Mafia.

One night, a young man named John Gallagher decided to make the walk from Betula in search of entertainment, as Clermont tended to have a much livelier social scene. Instead, he encountered two men at the tile plant, firing a kiln. For some reason, the two workers at the factory took offense at Gallagher's presence. A fight broke out, and Gallagher fell wounded from three bullet wounds in his back. He later died from his injuries. One of the workers, Christi Peters, was arrested and convicted of the crime. At his conviction, it was determined that he was insane. He lived out his years at the Warren State Hospital.

The first church in Clermont, the Clermont Union Congregational Church, was built by the Buffalo Coal Company. Later, it was joined by the Saint Sabinas Catholic Church in 1895 and the Clermont Methodist Church in 1898.

As in any town in that era, illness was a serious matter in the days before cutting-edge technology and high-tech health care. A diphtheria epidemic swept through Clermont in 1909. Many children died during the scourge. One family lost five children in just over twenty days.

The factory eventually was destroyed by fire in November 1961 and was not rebuilt. The Kaul Clay fire was devastating to the town. During the horrific inferno, many residents were confident that the local fire department would be able to put the blaze out. There were fire hydrants located near the factory and a large pond behind it. But the local fire truck would not start for some reason and never made it to the scene. The locals and volunteers from neighboring communities converged on the scene and did the best they could to fight the blaze, but to no avail. The business was a total loss. As the company had a second factory in Ohio, it made no plans to rebuild. The loss of this major employer in the area sealed Clermont's fate, and residents began moving away.

The Town Today

Clermont is technically still a functioning community, although it has precious few residents. Many of the hunting camps in the area, which are clearly visible to visitors, are actually old company houses. Clermont Union Church and the community's school are also hunting camps today. The site of the Clermont Methodist Church is reportedly just east of the current Clermont Fire Hall. A small cemetery is located just east of the town, along the main road.

Directions

From Smethport, drive southwest on Route 6. Turn left onto Route 146 in Marvindale. Route 146 intersects with the SR 2001 in Clermont, which is marked by a stop sign.

North-Central Pennsylvania

SCOTIA

Located west of State College, in the Great Pine Barrens in Centre County, Scotia was the brainchild of famous philanthropist and industrialist Andrew Carnegie. He envisioned a model mining community, promising reliable employment and wealth to the area. To some degree, his dream was realized, as most residents were content, decently paid workers, at least in warm-weather months. The mines eventually ran bare, however, and the town died out.

History

The Scotia area was initially inhabited by Shawnee and Delaware Indians. Neither group stayed long, as the sandy soil in the area made growing even hardy crops difficult. The Indians went into the Barrens to search for medicinal herbs and other plants.

The land that included Scotia was purchased by white settlers in the mid-1700s. The vacating Indians pointed out places where iron ore was peeping out from the dirt, sand, and rock. But little was done about the wealth below the ground until 1784, when a sur-veyor named Joseph Wallis came upon a ridge of iron ore in the area. The land was quickly purchased by Col. John Patton and Col. Samuel Miles, who finally realized the importance of the iron banks below Scotia.

Prior to the mining operation, the first settlers who remained for any length of time were Abraham and John Hicks. Abraham obtained seventy acres of wilderness, cleared a homestead for himself, and built a log house and barn. He then built a blacksmith shop, which later became very busy after Andrew Carnegie founded the Scotia Iron Works.

The early mining in the area was mainly surface mining with picks and shovels. By necessity, this was seasonal work. When the ground became frozen in winter, work stopped, and so did the paychecks. Workers often lived in shanties and cabins and had to forage for food in the Barrens throughout the winter. It was perilous living in the Barrens. Not only was it easy to lose one's way in the cold and dark, but the threat from wild animals was ever present.

One night the mine foreman, John Henderson, was returning home after dark with his dog. A snow squall blew in, and Henderson lost the trail. He came upon a campfire burning and hunkered down for the night. In the fury of the storm, both man and dog became aware of a pair of eyes staring at them from the woods. Henderson grabbed a wooden club and raced at the unwelcome visitor. His dog also gave chase, and the sounds of a vicious animal fight could be heard above the roar of the blizzard.

The dog returned some time later, injured but alive. They barely slept the rest of the night and safely returned to the mine in the morn-ing. That day Henderson was informed of a large panther that had been stalking the campfire recently, no doubt attracted by the miners' food scraps. Shortly after that incident, a settler named James Ross found himself stalked in the Barrens by a black panther. It sprang at him but missed, and then disappeared into the brush.

Forest fires posed another threat to the settlers in the area. In 1869, a tar burner named Watkins noticed a fire burning in the direc-tion of his home. He raced to save his wife and children but arrived too late. He perished along with his family. The only survivor was the family dog, whose fur was singed off. The area where the cabin stood became known as Old Burnt Chimney.

Andrew Carnegie leased the ore rights in the area in 1881, when the town of Scotia really began. Carnegie named the town after his beloved native Scotland. He planned to make the town the ideal mining community and succeeded in this wish from 1881 until 1911, when the mines ran dry. (Although Carnegie ended his financial interest in the town in 1899, the community thrived for several more years.) Carnegie paid $90,000 for the lease of 365 acres plus the purchase of 135 acres of additional land, which later housed a huge ore washer and mud dam. At the time of the sale, the mining supervisor said, "Well, Andy, I hope you make a million dollars out of this deal." Carnegie replied, "I expect to make two million out of it." He exceeded that prediction by a handsome amount. At its peak, Scotia shipped 4,000 tons of iron ore a month.

Although viewed officially as one community, Scotia actually consisted of three sections: Scotia, Marysville, and River Hill. Marysville was initially known as West Scotia, but according to legend, it was renamed because so many women named Mary lived there.

Marysville consisted of fourteen single-family homes and three stores, all privately owned. Scotia had eleven double houses and one single home, in which the mine supervisor resided. River Hill had seven homes and a boardinghouse. River Hill and Scotia were company-owned. Five wells served the area, along with a blacksmith shop, cobbler, school, church, and general store.

The Rabbit Hill School was built in 1860. Up to ninety children at a time attended the one-room school, making it a challenge for the single teacher. It was a primary school only, and many of its graduates did not progress to high school. Education was valued in Scotia, however, and Carnegie donated $20 a month to the teacher's pay to ensure that the children of Scotia received a strong educational framework.

The townspeople of Scotia were fun-loving and actively sought out wholesome entertainment. The school building was often a place for lively social debates. Many of the town's residents looked forward to these debates between citizens as a recreational diversion. Dances were popular recreation in Scotia as well. At one point, there were four operating dance floors in Scotia, all of which were used almost nightly. Music was furnished by fiddle only, and talented fiddlers abounded. The dance floors were constructed outdoors, but when cold weather arrived, the dances were moved into private homes.

The Scotia Cornet Band was a great source of pride and was in great demand to play at festivals and picnics. When Andrew Carnegie visited the mine superintendent, Frank Clemson, the band marched down to serenade him. Carnegie was so moved and impressed that he told his host he would supply new instruments to as many of the band as wanted them. Thus the Scotia Cornet Band was outfitted in grand style by the Carnegie Steel Company.

The people of Scotia were well known in the area for their practical jokes. One of the more famous gags was a bucket of filthy water atop a tipple above a road into town used by many peddlers. The bucket was located at the corner of the shoemaker's shop and was difficult to see from the road. One peddler was enraged by his damp welcome to town and started up the steps to the tipple, in an effort to confront his tormentors. As he advanced, the men threw bucket upon bucket of water at him. With great effort, the peddler arrived at the top of the tipple and began to threaten the men. In response, they offered to help him clean up by throwing him into the ore washer. The peddler beat a hasty retreat.

The fun ended when the men accidentally doused the mine superintendent. The contrite culprits were allowed to keep their jobs but were ordered to stop pulling such pranks.

Although generally a peaceful place, crime did touch Scotia. Bert Delige was a convicted murderer and rapist. Bert was the grandson of Aaron Delige, the unofficial leader of the large black population of Scotia, which was said to number sixty at one point. Besides having a long history of petty crime and holdups, Bert spent three years in Western Pennsylvania Penitentiary for the shooting death of thirteen-year-old neighbor Ralph Williams. Even as he stood with his head in the hangman's noose for another crime, Bert Delige swore that the shooting of the boy was accidental.

He confessed to the other crime, however, and was proven guilty. On October 17, 1910, a quiet fall evening, residents of Scotia had heard children crying and gone to investigate. They found two young children standing over the body of their mother, whose throat had been cut. Mrs. Baudis had been slashed with a razor.

Combined with a mountain of evidence, Bert Delige's confession to the crime sealed his fate. He was hanged on April 25, 1911, the last hanging to occur at the Centre County Jail in Bellefonte. Bert's mother begged to have him buried in the Scotia Cemetery. Permission was granted for the family to bury him just beyond its boundaries.

Not surprisingly, there were several fatal accidents at the Scotia Mines. One occurred when Samuel Saxion was stirring material at the ore washer. He took a step to speak to a man on a platform above him. Just then, the man above accidentally dislodged a chunk of dirt, which landed on the board on which Saxion stood, surprising him. He lost his balance and fell into the ore washer. The alarm was sounded immediately, but the machine continued to turn before it could be stopped. Although Saxion surprised the crowd by surviving the initial event, he died at his home later that night. He is buried at Gray's Cemetery in Buffalo Run Valley. Time has worn his headstone to near illegibility, but it reads, "A loving husband, a father dear. A faithful friend lies buried here."

On April 30, 1894, one of the few suicides occurred in Scotia. John McMullen, who had been hired by Andrew Carnegie to clear the land for the ore washer, hanged himself from the roof of his cabin. He had suffered from severe stomach pains from the use of a faulty medication, which he treated with laudanum. He quickly became addicted to the laudanum. After receiving minimal help for his addiction through Poor District, an early form of welfare, and being shuttled from relative to relative, he returned to his cabin in Scotia. He had recently begun to improve his life, working at picking flint in the ore washer, when he committed suicide. He also is buried in Gray's Cemetery.

Along with flagging mine outputs, Andrew Carnegie became concerned about the constant threat of forest fires in the Scotia area. Such fires were a common threat in the Barrens and wrought havoc with the wooden structures that formed the infrastructure of Scotia. After witnessing two such fires, Carnegie had had enough. He decided to sell his stake in Scotia to the Bellefonte Furnace Company in 1899. The selling price was $65,000.

Work at the site slowly dwindled over the next several years. By 1923, everyone but "Mayor" Wilson Ghaner had left Scotia. Ghaner lived there for his entire life, until his death in 1933. While he was the sole occupant of the town, he continued to send news items to the local newspapers about his beloved hometown, believing that the town should remain alive.

The Town Today

Scotia lies west of State College. A town currently exists with that name, consisting mostly of a bedroom community of housing developments serving State College. It is just west of Route 322 on Scotia Road. Marysville lies just west of the current Scotia town. No standing structures remain, but foundations of the furnace and some of the houses survive.

The Centre Furnace, which played a role in smelting the iron ore from Scotia, stands today on Route 26 outside State College. A small historical society museum is located on-site, staffed by friendly curators.

The Scotia Cemetery is located in what today is a private backyard in Marysville. At this time, only one headstone remains, although reportedly a dozen bodies are buried there. The remaining headstone is that of Aaron Delige. The other graves in the cemetery belong to six white citizens and five other black citizens, buried near Delige. The grave of his convicted grandson, Bert, is marked by a gathering of flat stones that can still be found today.

Directions

From State College, take Route 220 south/Route 322 west toward Lewistown. Exit to the left in .7 mile on Gray's Woods Boulevard. Follow this road .4 mile to Scotia Road. Make a left. Foundations can be found scattered around the area.

REVELTON, EAGLETON, PEACOCK, AND ROCK CABIN

These four ghost towns in Clinton County are grouped together, not because they are individually insignificant, but because their histories are so interwoven.

History

The history of Clinton County was profoundly influenced by the presence and industry of John Reaville, who was hired by wealthy landowners, the Potters, to supervise new mines in the Clinton County area. A rather stern man with a commanding air, Reaville was a native of Nottingham, England, and had a great talent for business as well as mining. The men who worked for him had great respect for this brusque Englishman.

By 1854, Reaville had overseen a successful mine operation on the Tangascootac Creek, which was named Reavilletown. The name was later simplified to Revelton. Soon Reaville had added three other mining operations in the area: Eagleton, Peacock, and Rock Cabin. The mining towns were all located within a few miles of one another, which made overseeing them a manageable task for Reaville.

The mines in Clinton County were successful, although the employees did not always reap the benefits of that windfall. The mine workers at Eagleton became disgruntled with the small percentage of profit they were being paid, compared with the fortunes that the owners and managers were raking in from the mining operations. They declared a strike, the first in the bituminous coal-mining industry in Pennsylvania.

Reaville was no shrinking violet in the face of the strike. He sent word to Lock Haven. The sheriff responded, bringing with him a band of more than a dozen armed deputies to disband the strike in Eagleton. In the face of such adversity, the strikers peacefully dispersed. The breakup of the Eagleton strike helped cement Reaville's reputation as a tough manager. His reputation for occasional brutality toward his workers became the stuff of legend.

Initially Reaville lived in the rough towns in which he worked. He soon tired of rustic living, however, and purchased more than 3,500 acres on the top of the mountain, where he built a mansion styled after the English manor homes of his childhood. Once completed, the mansion was the site of many raucous parties. Reaville was widely known for his love of liquor, which flowed freely at his galas.

The town of Revelton had about twenty houses, as well as a school, company store, livery stable, and blacksmith shop. The Revelton Iron Furnace was opened around 1865. Unfortunately, the poor quality of the coal in the area made the furnace somewhat unnecessary and unusable, and it closed down in less than a year.

Eagleton, founded in 1853, was much harder to access than the other towns. About ten miles northeast of Revelton, it was positioned high up on the mountain, making rail service to remove the mined coal difficult. It eventually encompassed more than fifty houses, a company office, a store, and several outbuildings.

Peacock, founded in 1865, got its name from the odd green-blue color of the bituminous coal mined in the area. At Peacock's height, there were more than fifty houses in the town, in addition to a huge boardinghouse accommodating eighty people. Peacock was rather long-lived, remaining inhabited through the early 1930s.

Rock Cabin was abandoned in 1870 after the mines closed. At its peak, it held almost 100 homes and a large mining operation.

Reaville died at age seventy-one of heart disease, in 1876. Rumors circulated, and continue to this day, that he buried a fortune in his basement before his death. The house burned in 1894, and it is unclear whether the treasure existed, and if so, whether it had been found.

The Towns Today

Revelton is the most interesting of these present-day ghost towns. Foundations of the Reaville Mansion remain, as do foundations of other houses in the area. Reliable sources report that the iron forge still stands just south of the Tangascootac Creek, although repeated trips to the area have not uncovered it.

Little exists of the other towns, unfortunately. It is reported that some foundations and other evidence can be found if you search closely. Near the top of the mountain, among many pine trees, is a line of oak trees planted by John Reaville. The Sproul State Forest created a hiking trail, named the Eagleton Mine Camp Trail, which covers much of the area where these sites are located.

Directions

You can reach Revelton by taking Route 150 to Beech Creek from Lock Haven. Turn right just before you come to the bridge, onto Monument-Orviston Road. Bear right onto Beech Creek Road. Follow it for several miles, then turn right onto Peacock Road. Turn right onto Revelton Road, which is a fairly rugged dirt road, to drive toward Revelton. At the wooden sign for Revelton, you must leave your car and hike a couple miles to the site. As you approach the Tangascootac Creek, you can find some of the house foundations along the sides of the trail and hidden in the woods. The elusive iron forge should lie to the east of the trail. The Reaville Mansion foundations are located shortly past the creek, as you climb the mountain. Return to Beech Creek Road, and head northwest. Eagleton Road is on your right and will lead you to the Eagleton site.

Peacock and Rock Cabin are located in the Sproul State Forest, along the Eagleton Mine Camp Trail. To reach the trail, take Route 120 west from Lock Haven for about 7 miles, and turn left onto Eagleton Road. You can park at the eastern trailhead at the intersection of Eagleton Road and the Eagleton Railroad Trail. The western trailhead can be found where Shear Trap Trail meets Eagleton Road.

ALVIRA

Nestled behind the Allenwood Federal Prison outside of Lewisburg, in Union County, lie the remnants of this picturesque little village.

History

Alvira was founded around 1825 and was initially named Wisetown. It was located in the northwest corner of Gregg Township, three miles west of Allenwood. At its peak, around 1900, approximately 100 people called Alvira home.

Alvira boasted a blacksmith shop, school, post office, several shops, and three churches—Baptist, Presbyterian, and Messiah. In time, an auto repair shop and a baseball field were added to the area. The townspeople were a close-knit group and tended to stay long-term in the area. In fact, the owner of the auto repair shop was the last remaining resident of Alvira. He finally left in June 1942, when a tornado tore the roof off his home.

The United States had entered World War II a few months before talk of building a munitions plant reached the residents of Alvira, in the White Deer Valley. On March 7, 1942, a town meeting was called, held in the Stone Church in nearby Montgomery. Government officials at the meeting explained the plans to build a munitions storage facility in Alvira, which would mean taking over fifty farms. The 8,000-acre buyout happened quickly. Within a week, the issue was decided, leaving some residents outraged and fearful.

Petitions were circulated by some, decrying the project and its impact on the residents of the valley, but to no avail. The secrecy surrounding the project worked against the locals. It was considered dangerous to discuss the details of the proposed munitions factory, as they might fall into the wrong hands. The fight to stop the government's decision fell on deaf ears.

Eventually the townspeople dutifully packed up and left their homes, scattering around the state. Despite the resistance by some, many left proudly, viewing the move as a patriotic one that allowed for the war effort to be more effective. Many stayed in the general area, putting down new roots in Lewisburg, Montgomery, and other nearby towns. In all, 177 homes were abandoned and destroyed in Alvira.

The government decided to build an enormous $15 million trinitrotoluene (TNT) factory to supply the army with explosives. The proposed plant would employ more than 10,000 workers in the building phase, and then 4,000 to actually manufacture the TNT.

A bus ran between Alvira and Williamsport to transport workers. A trailer park was set aside nearby to house employees. Storage bunkers were built to hold the explosives. The storage huts, which resemble concrete igloos, were built with thick walls, designed to explode upward rather than outward in case of accidental explosion. In addition, the Army Corps of Engineers built a sewage treatment plant, two water treatment plants, and paved roads to accommodate the factory. It appeared that the government was prepared to produce an enormous quantity of explosives, and that the people of Alvira had done their patriotic duty by leaving the area.

The administration building at Alvira was erected and open by June 1942, and work began at the plant in earnest. But despite the workers' enthusiasm and hard work, the TNT was produced only in small amounts. It turned out the War Department did not have the voracious need for TNT that the government had expected. The TNT factory was abandoned after functioning for just a short time, and the storage bunkers were emptied. By late 1945, all work had stopped, and the only remaining residents were security guards.

This left the former residents scratching their heads, wondering why they had been forced to leave their lifelong homes, which were subsequently destroyed. Why had such an expensive, destructive undertaking been such a folly? The people who lived in the White Deer Valley tended to be a hardy lot, however, and for the most part, they got on with their lives.

Any rancor that remains rests in the broken promises that were made to the residents of Alvira. When they were told of the decision to demolish their town to build the munitions plant, the homeowners were also told that when the need for TNT ended, they would be given first rights to buy back their original lands. This never happened. Instead, the land was kept by the federal government to build a prison, with portions sold to the state of Pennsylvania for game lands. Still, many of the displaced residents were at peace with the decisions that had been made. The general attitude was that it was better to have had the munitions plant built, even if it was not needed, than for the army to have needed the explosives but had no way to get them.

The Town Today

The site of Alvira is now contained within Pennsylvania State Game Lands 252. Please use caution if visiting this site during hunting season. The land contains a great deal of wildlife, such as bears, deer, turkeys, ducks, pheasants, grouse, and foxes.

It is not possible to tour the fabulous TNT plant, as it now lies behind the fence of the Allenwood Federal Prison. It was converted to a prison farm and now accommodates more than 100 minimum-security prisoners.

The ordnance bunkers dot the trails and woods around Alvira. The ammunition once stored in them is gone, but the igloo-shaped structures now serve as storage units for the Game Commission and for local farmers who lease fields within the game lands. The farmers have agreed to give the Game Commission half of their harvested crops as rent. The Game Commission, in turn, uses the grain to provide emergency deer feed in winter and for feeding the animals at the game farms around the state.

Two cemeteries remain intact: the Washington Presbyterian Church Cemetery and the Alvira Cemetery. Both have church foundations adjacent to the graveyards. Impressive stone gates erected before 1790 greet the visitor to the Washington Presbyterian cemetery, located just north of the fence delineating the Allenwood Federal Prison. The Alvira Cemetery is a little more than a quarter mile north of the Presbyterian cemetery on Alvira Road. Church foundations lie near the road, slightly east of the older part of the cemetery.

One of the more intriguing gravestones in the Washington Presbyterian yard is that of the Sechler family. It stands watch over the remains of John Sechler (1808–88), Anna Marie Sechler (1813–90), their infant son (March 1855), John Sedam Sechler (1834–60), and Elias Sechler (1838–76). A special encasement within the stone has this inscription: "Beneath this granite slab lies a confederate bullet with which Elias Sechler, member of the 131st Regiment Pennsylvania Volunteer Infantry was wounded in the charge made on Marye's Heights by General Humphrey's division at the Battle of Fredericksburg, Virginia. December 13, 1862."

It is surprisingly easy to get lost while exploring Alvira. The trails in the area are cut in a grid pattern, and the intersections look similar to each other. The munitions bunkers also look alike, leaving few landmarks to orient visitors. Pay close attention to your location when visiting.

Directions

From Route 15, take Route 54 west to Elimsport Road, and make a right. Take a left onto Alvira Road. After approximately a mile, the road surface turns to gravel. Follow the road to the end, where you will see the Washington Presbyterian Church Cemetery gates on your left. Park and explore the church's foundations. Return approximately a quarter of a mile on Alvira Road and see the foundations of Messiah Church, with its adjacent cemetery.

FORT ANTES

Fort Antes, in Lycoming County, was presided over by a courageous soldier whose protection of the nearby settlers helped enable the American frontier to hold strong against Indian attacks.

History

Fort Antes was built in 1777 by Col. John Henry Antes. Situated across from present-day Jersey Shore, it was placed on a plateau overlooking the Nippenose Creek to optimize visual surveillance of the area, which was inhabited by Indians.

Colonel Antes was a respected man in both military and civil affairs. He had been a justice of the peace and sheriff in Northumberland County. As the frequency and destructiveness of Indian attacks increased, he was commissioned to the rank of lieutenant colonel of the 4th Battalion of the Militia of Northumberland County in May 1777.

Antes initially had constructed a gristmill on the site around 1773. The gristmill was of enormous benefit to the settlers in the area, providing them with flour made from wheat and corn grown nearby. It is difficult in modern times to imagine how difficult making even a simple loaf of bread could be, with no easy supply of flour. A gristmill therefore made the area surrounding it a desirable place to settle.

Colonel Antes's commission required him to attempt to secure the frontier against Indian attacks. The Indians had been attacking the local settlers randomly, and there was some talk of abandoning the frontier altogether. The colonel was to provide some protection for the settlers and attempt to intimidate the hostile Indian population with a military presence in the area.

In 1777, he built Fort Antes on a bluff overlooking the West Branch of the Susquehanna River to protect the gristmill and the settlers, but also because the location provided a view of the path used by Indians to travel up Lycoming Creek. The path was often used by war parties who attacked local settlements with great viciousness. The vantage point allowed the settlers to have some advance warning of raids and take defensive actions.

The fort was ten to twelve feet high, with indentations cut into the wood to accommodate musket barrels. It is believed that the fort contained a cannon brought from Fort Muncy to intimidate the Indians. This has never been verified, although a cannonball was found many years later below the hill on the riverbank, supporting the theory.

Besides serving to protect the settlers, the fort also provided some refuge for the Fair Play Men, a group of white men who lived across the river in Indian territory. Living beyond the border of American territory placed them outside the jurisdiction of the laws of the Pennsylvania Colonial government. Essentially, they were illegal squatters in the area around the West Branch of the Susquehanna River. Instead of following American laws, they constructed their own system, which involved three elected commissioners whose duties included ruling on land claims and other legal issues. In an astonishing coincidence, the Fair Play Men devised a Declaration of Independence from Great Britain on exactly the same day the American Declaration of Independence was signed in Philadelphia, July 4, 1776. The Fair Play Men's declaration was signed beneath the "Tiadaghton Elm" on the shore of Pine Creek not far from Fort Antes and is largely viewed by history as a superb piece of legislation.

By all accounts, the winter of 1777–78 was particularly harrowing for the settlers of the Nippenose area, where Fort Antes was located. The number of surprise attacks by the Indians reached a peak during that time. First a settler was murdered and scalped by Indians at the mouth of Pine Creek, just beyond sight of the fort, on December 23. The other settlers were horrified to realize how close to safety the man had been when he fell. They subsequently became more vigilant and tried to remain as close to the safety of the fort as possible. On January 1, another man died in a similar manner, however, murdered and scalped a short distance from the fort. A few deaths may not seem significant, but there were relatively few settlers along the frontier line in Pennsylvania, and the loss of even a few was a difficult blow to the communities living in constant fear of attack.

One of the most dramatic Indian attacks occurred in June 1777, when two women decided to cross the river in canoes to milk their cows, which were grazing in pastures there. Four armed civilian men, including their husbands, accompanied them. When they reached the shore, they found only one of the cows near the creek. The other cow's bell rang faintly in the distance. Zephaniah Miller, Abel Cady, and James Armstrong set off to find her and drive her in toward shore for milking. They left Isaac Bouser with the women, who were milking the first cow. The men did not realize that Indians were hiding the cow, ringing the bell, and lying in wait.

As the settlers entered the woods, they were set upon by the warriors, who viciously scalped them and flung their bodies to the ground. Two of the men lay bleeding and dying. Armstrong was injured in the back of the head but was able to escape, firing his weapon at the Indians, which alarmed the warriors enough to stop pursuing him. He raced to reach the river. Meanwhile, Bouser and the women, hearing the shots, quickly hid themselves in the underbrush.

At the fort, the soldiers also heard the shots and prepared to rush to their assistance. Colonel Antes ordered them to stay in the fort, as the Indians might have set up another ambush that would leave the fort vulnerable to being overrun. But the men disobeyed orders, anxious to help the desperate settlers.

Fortunately, the rescue party met no appreciable resistance from the Indians and successfully rescued the two women and Bouser. Armstrong was also evacuated to the fort, where he died several days later in agony from his wounds. The men found Cady and Miller dead where they had fallen and buried them. The rescuers pursued the attacking Indians but were unable to capture them. After firing at them as they retreated, the men found blood on the ground, suggesting that some of the warriors had been injured.

Not all Indians in the area were hostile to the settlers, however. One in particular, called Job Chilloway, was a Delaware Indian who had converted to Christianity through the Moravian faith. He was a respected, trusted friend to the settlers and soldiers in the area, who depended on the information that he clandestinely gave them regarding raids being planned. He is particularly notable as the first messenger to let the white settlers know that a massive, orchestrated attack was being planned all along the frontier, which led to an evacuation known as the Big Runaway in the summer of 1778.

During the Big Runaway, Fort Antes and the other forts along the frontier line were evacuated, as the soldiers and settlers made their way to Fort Augusta in present-day Northumberland County. Within a month of the retreat, armed soldiers made their way back up the valley to Fort Muncy, bravely surveying the damage that the marauding Indian war parties had done. From there, Colonial scouts traveled to Fort Antes, arriving soon after the Indians had sacked the place. The mill and homes had been burned to the ground. The fort still stood, as the heavy oak timbers resisted the Indians' attempts to burn them. The area was deemed ready for inhabitation by the returning settlers.

Colonel Antes went back to the fort with some of the settlers, but no militia accompanied him. The residents of the area were frightened, anxious that the lack of a military presence at the fort would make them vulnerable again to attack. Colonel Antes assured them that the fort would continue to be a place of refuge and implored the settlers to remain in the area. He was successful in convincing them. The fort continued to be used for defense by the nearby settlers, until the problems with the local Indians ended permanently.

When peace was established, the fort was abandoned and allowed to decay. Colonel Antes rebuilt the gristmill and continued to supply the area with needed flour. During his life, the colonel had two wives, thirteen children, and many grandchildren. After his death in May 1820 at age eighty-three, he was buried in the graveyard near the site of the old fort. His grave, unfortunately, remains unmarked. Along with him in the cemetery are the bodies of Cady, Miller, and Armstrong, killed by Indians in an attack.

The Fort Today

Fort Antes was located near the current town of Antes Fort, in Lycoming County. It stood on the southeast side of the West Branch of the Susquehanna River. Little is left of the actual fort or mill, although some report that remnants of foundations can be found on the hill overlooking the river.

Directions

From Williamsport, take Route 220 west to Jersey Shore. Take Route 44 east and cross the West Branch of the Susquehanna River. After the second portion of the river, turn right on Old Fort Road, before you reach the current town of Antes Fort. The fort and gristmill were located along this road, overlooking the river.

FORT AUGUSTA

Fort Augusta, in Northumberland County, played a critical role in the settlement and defense of the citizens of Pennsylvania in the mid-1700s.

History

Fort Augusta was built in 1756 as a British fort in an attempt to defend the region from attack during the French and Indian War. From the end of that war until the beginning of the Revolutionary

War, the fort served as a significant trading post between Indians and settlers in Pennsylvania.

When the Revolutionary War began, the fort took on a new role. It functioned as an American stronghold against the Indians, who were well armed by the British in an attempt to rout the Americans living on the frontier. Fort Augusta was the base of operations for a line of frontier forts that stretched north up the Susquehanna River and some of its tributary creeks.

Fort Augusta was solidly constructed, undoubtedly contributing to its usefulness as a key frontier defensive position. It was built with logs standing vertically on the front side facing the Susquehanna River and logs lashed horizontally at the rear of the fort. A dry moat ran along the front. A bastion extended on each corner, allowing the inhabitants to defend all walls in a crossfire mode.

In all, the fort consisted of six interconnected buildings, making it a substantial structure compared with most frontier forts of that time. The soldiers and officers made their quarters within the 4,000-square-foot structure. The fort reportedly contained as many as sixteen cannons, and the powder magazine was built into the basement area.

Ironically, its very presence, which exuded strength and confidence, made it a poor target for attack. In its tenure, Fort Augusta was never put under siege, and most attacks were easily repelled. It was the smaller frontier forts that were targets of Indian attacks.

Col. Samuel Hunter was commander of the fort during the Revolutionary War era. He commanded the Northumberland County Militia, which provided protection and defense as needed to all of the northern frontier forts and stockades.

Perhaps the most famous function of Fort Augusta was its role in the Big Runaway in 1778. Upon hearing of a massive, coordinated Indian attack in the works, all of the frontier forts were evacuated, with the assigned militia and locals fleeing to Fort Augusta. Although many of the outlying forts' inhabitants returned to the north within a few months of the horrific raids, some remained in the Sunbury and Shamokin Dam area.

After the conclusion of the Revolutionary War, Colonel Hunter was granted permission to take up permanent residence at the fort. He purchased the surrounding land and built a mansion near the fort. The fort itself was dismantled in 1794, leaving only the powder magazine and well, which remain to this day. Colonel Hunter's family inhabited the mansion for generations, until it was destroyed by fire in 1848. Another house was built on the same spot in 1852, and it still stands today.

The Fort Today

Today the site of Fort Augusta is located at 1150 N. Front St., in Sunbury, Northumberland County. The Hunter House stands on the site of the old fort and is now a museum administered by the Northumberland County Historical Society. The museum contains a collection of artifacts from the fort and the outlying area. Within Hunter House is a genealogical library, which contains a great number of detailed records on the early inhabitants of the county. The museum is typically open on Monday, Wednesday, and Friday afternoons.

Directions

From Route 15, take Route 61 south toward Sunbury. Take the Route 61 S./Route 147 N. ramp toward Sunbury/Front Street. Take a slight left onto Route 147 north. Proceed to the Hunter House museum at 1125 N. Front St., which is well marked.

MASTEN

Once a busy lumber town, Masten is slowly disappearing into the forest of Lycoming County.

History

Masten (also seen as Maston) was founded in the early 1900s by Sen. Charles W. Sones as a town to house the workers for his lumbermill and tannery. It had some ninety homes, a hotel, boardinghouse, dance hall, barbershop, and pool room.

No liquor was permitted within the company town, although the Molnick brothers operated a popular still out in the mountains. The Molnicks were troublemakers of long standing. After running a profitable still for several years, they decided that they needed greater booty and stole the Masten safe, for which they were later arrested. The money was recovered and spent years later by a cellmate of one of the Molnicks, who had been given a map to the location of the money. It had been buried in two mason jars under a log next to Dry Run. The cellmate found approximately $2,700 in the jars. He then took the cash to Philadelphia and sold the outdated bills to other outlaws there, as they could not be redeemed at face value at the banks.

Masten is typically described as a genial, pleasant town in which to live. Unlike many other lumber towns of the era, there was no history of riots, fights, or other rowdy behavior. The residents enjoyed their local band, dances, watching baseball on the town diamond, and fishing for trout in Pleasant Stream.

The company store sold almost everything imaginable, from clothespins to full suits of clothing to fresh fruit and eggs. Like most company stores, the Masten store was a hub for the community, with the sawmill workers often meeting at the counter to socialize after their shifts.

The houses in town rented from the company for about $5 a month. Most of them had three rooms upstairs and three downstairs. Some of the more rustic homes had plain wood walls, which the inhabitants often covered with fabric or wallpaper. Some of the newer homes had actual plastered walls. None of the houses were painted, which was typical in company towns.

Gardens were very common in Masten, with almost every family growing their own vegetables. Because the local cows were allowed to roam freely, most families fenced in their gardens to keep the hungry bovines from devouring them.

The town was the hub for many lumber camps scattered around the area, where many of the wood hicks lived. The accommodations in the camps were somewhat rougher than the houses in town. The wood hicks bathed infrequently and led a rather rough existence. They loved their fun and looked forward to each payday, when they descended upon town, spent every dime they had made, and then disappeared back into the mountains.

Masten was in business for approximately twenty-five years, until the lumbermill and tannery closed in September 1930. The town was quickly abandoned as workers moved on to other employment. Later, a CCC camp was located at the site but closed after ten years.

The Town Today

The foundations of the enormous sawmill can still be seen near Pleasant Stream. When you look at them, the sheer size of the operation becomes evident. Foundations of several houses lie scattered around the area near the mill. Some of the deer-hunting camps standing near the sawmill foundations are actually some of the homes from the days of Masten. A stone fireplace and chimney built by the CCC is located near the sawmill remains and is easily spotted from the road.

Directions

From Platt, in Sullivan County, follow SR 4006 past Shunk, where it turns into SR 4002. At Tomkins Corners, turn left onto T398, keeping right, until you see the CCC sign and chimney on your left. There is a small sign in Tomkins Corners pointing the way.

FORT REED

One of the more intriguing mysteries in Clinton County surrounds the actual location of a Revolutionary War–era fort, Fort Reed. A successful local business had been built around claims that the fort lay on its site, but a recent find in the Clinton County Historical Society's own backyard may change the way historians look at Lock Haven.

History

Fort Reed (also known as Fort Reid) was erected in the 1770s in what is now Lock Haven. The fort, built by William Reed, was the westernmost in a line of defensive stockades along a frontier stretching to Fort Augusta in what is now Sunbury.

William Reed was born in 1740 in Donegal, Ireland. He emigrated with his family to the American colonies in 1747. He later married, and he and his wife had ten children while in Pennsylvania: five girls and five boys.

In 1778, the Indians living in Pennsylvania planned a major coordinated attack on the fortified line of defenses that the settlers had erected. The settlers learned of the imminent attack in time and fled en masse to Fort Augusta. This event became known as the Big Runaway.

The Big Runaway is one of the more disturbing accounts of the state of war between the settlers and their Indian foes, who were well supplied with weapons and ammunition by the British. There were friendly Indians in the area as well, who at times provided great assistance to the settlers. As the attacks of the Big Runaway were starting, a chief who had befriended the Reed family raced to warn them. As he neared the fort, nervous settlers shot at him, wounding him. Mrs. Reed recognized the chief and had him brought into the fort, where she gently tended his wounds. When he regained consciousness, he told her of the coming attack. The settlers immediately packed and fled. Other accounts record a more horrifying ending to this tale, saying that a bigoted settler then shot and killed the chief. History is unclear which version is true.

In an earlier episode, the Reeds' daughter Jane made her way to the dairy to milk the cows. While hard at her task, she looked up to find herself surrounded by Native American warriors, who brandished tomahawks. Instead of murdering her, they began chanting a song and danced around her while waving their axes. Although frightened, she was also puzzled. They had ample opportunity to kill her but did not do so. They eventually departed, and she ran back to the fort.

The next day, Jane decided to test a theory that she had devised. On her way to milk the cows, she grabbed several tin mugs and carried them to the cowshed. Her hunch was correct. The warriors returned and began their threatening dance around her. She filled a mug with warm milk and passed it to a brave. He stopped dancing and accepted it. She then filled mugs for the others, who also drank deeply. They returned the cups and disappeared into the woods.

Each day they repeated this ritual, returning for a cup of milk from the young woman. The chief who later attempted to warn the Reeds of the impending attack was one of these thirsty men.

After the Big Runaway, the Reeds spent several years in exile in Sunbury and then in Chester County. They had no way of knowing whether their beloved home still stood. In the 1780s, after several years in exile, they returned. Miraculously, the fort and the Reeds' log home were essentially intact and were quickly made habitable again. The local settlers began to trickle back into the area, albeit warily. Some chose to remain in safer territory.

Militia soldiers provided the defense of Fort Reed and also scouted for Indian activity. The fort was an important structure to the local settlers, as it provided defense and shelter for the area between the Bald Eagle Valley and the White Deer Creek along the Susquehanna River. The hope was that the fort would hold the line against the Indians, and that the white settlers would continue to prosper and maintain the current frontier line.

The Reeds never owned the land on which Fort Reed stood. Instead, it was owned by John Fleming. In later years, the land was sold to Jerry Church, an illustrious man who founded Lock Haven.

The Fort Today

The actual location of Fort Reed is hotly contested in Clinton County. A successful restaurant at the Grafius House claimed that it was built on the site of Fort Reed, and a monument erected supported that claim. A review of historical documents, however, supports the contention that newly found stone foundations may tell the true story of the location of the fort.

The Clinton County Historical Society is housed in the Heisey House, on East Water Street in Lock Haven. The society discovered the foundations in the museum's backyard, and a team of archaeologists is currently working to determine the veracity of the claims. Several reliable historical sources certainly support the theory that this was indeed the location of the fort.

The Heisey House is open from 10 A.M. to 4 P.M. Tuesday through Friday. Please check with the curator before venturing to the possible fort location behind the house.

The site of the Reeds' log cabin is located approximately where the Hotel Meitzler is today in Lock Haven.

Directions

From Route 220, take Route 120 toward Lock Haven/Renovo. Turn right onto Water Street. The Heisey House is located at 362 E. Water Street. The Hotel Meitzler is located approximately .5 mile west of Water Street.

KEATING

Are there secret silver mines hidden near the former town of Keating in Clinton County?

History

White settlers began making their homes in the Keating area in the late 1760s on land that was owned by the Iroquois nation. The Iroquois warned the settlers several times to leave the area but were ignored. Thus began a series of vicious raids, which culminated in a series of ferocious battles in 1778 and 1779.

In late 1778, most of the area's population of settlers evacuated the area of the West Branch of the Susquehanna River to escape imminent slaughter by the Indians. This became known as the Big Runaway. The people fled to nearby forts and stockades, and most made their way south to Fort Augusta in modern Northumberland.

Another evacuation known as the Little Runaway began in 1779, as Gen. John Sullivan led his forces to quell the Iroquois violence in the Keating area. The settlers again fled their homes, many of which were destroyed by the Iroquois and the British, who were advancing to meet General Sullivan in battle.

In 1784, a treaty called the Last Purchase was signed in New York between the United States and the Six Nations of the Iroquois, transferring the remaining Indian Territory to the state of Pennsylvania. The purchase was later ratified by both the Delaware and Wyandot tribes. Settlers began to move into the area in earnest.

Rumors of great deposits of silver in the area brought some settlers hoping to strike it rich. These stories were based on reports that settlers had seen Indians carrying great bags of silver ore from the mountains to their canoes on the Sinnemahoning River. White settlers were never able to find the silver mines. To this day, rumors continue to circulate about the existence of the lost mines.

The Keating Hotel was built and became a hub for the community. A four-story structure, it could house up to fifty people in its rooms. It was also a popular meeting place where locals could congregate and socialize. A local store provided for the material needs of the townspeople.

Residents of the area were a diverse lot: lumberjacks, immigrant railroad workers and miners, mountain men, hunters, and men working on transporting lumber down the river. They were a hardy, rough-and-tumble bunch, which made for a lively town. In addition, a small community of African Americans lived for some time in the Keating area. Oral tradition stated that they were runaway slaves who had come to the area by way of the Underground Railroad, but documentation is scarce.

Of interesting note, just across the creek from the hotel, a railroad engineer found petroglyphs on a rock ledge, left by ancient Indians in the area. There were renditions of birds and animals, as well as a map of the local area. It appeared to be a guide to the local game in the area and where the animals could be found in great numbers.

A murder mystery continues to circulate among the few remaining people living in the Keating area. Legend tells of how Dolf Rhone's wife left him abruptly for the doctor of a nearby town. The same night that she left, Dolf disappeared, and the Rhones' boiler was fired up for the first time in years. Many still wonder whether Dolf was disposed of in the boiler so that Mrs. Rhone was free to leave with her lover. Dolf was never seen again, and the mystery remains unsolved.

The town gradually deteriorated as the years passed. A series of major floods throughout the late 1880s and the 1900s took its toll on Keating. The water washed away homes and eroded cemeteries. The hotel closed, and most residents drifted away.

The Town Today

A few homes still stand in the Keating area, most now used as hunting camps or retreats. The hotel and railroad depot are gone, both destroyed, although the foundations of the hotel remain. If you hike up the Sinnemahoning from Keating, you can glimpse the ghost hamlet of Wistar, of which only portions of the train depot are left, indicated by a concrete railroad marker.

Just across the creek from Keating, high on the hill, is a small cemetery. Look for a wooden sign and a small parking area. It is definitely worth a visit.

Directions

Follow Route 120 west from Renovo, in Clinton County. The turnoff for Keating/Pottersdale Road is on the left, about 3 miles beyond Cooks Run.

FORT FREELAND

Fort Freeland, in Northumberland County, was the site of a devastating battle between the Pennsylvania settlers and a force of more than 300 British soldiers and Indian allies.

History

Fort Freeland was initially built as a gristmill along the Warrior Run Creek, approximately four miles before it meets the Susquehanna River. It was built in 1773–74 by Jacob Freeland and several other families. The settlers enjoyed friendly relations with the local Indian population for several years. Around 1777, these relations began to sour, as they did all along the American frontier. As the Indian activity became more frightening, the families briefly left the area for safety. When they bravely returned in 1778, the families quickly built a twelve-foot-high stockade around the Freeland home, which consisted of a large log structure. The fort enclosed about half an acre of land. The gate was locked by bars from the inside.

Despite occasional mild skirmishes with the Indians, little damage was done to the Pennsylvania settlers for some time. The local residents breathed a sigh of relief. But that all changed in 1779.

On July 21, several of the male settlers were working in the cornfield behind the fort. They were set upon by a warring party of Indians around 9 A.M. Three of the settlers were killed and two were taken prisoner, including Ben Vincent, a ten-year-old boy. Ben was unaware of the fate of the others, including a brother, until an Indian shoved his brother's scalp into his face that afternoon.

At the time, the fort was protected by only twenty-one men, and they had precious little ammunition. The Indians, on the other hand, were well supplied with bullets from their British allies. The women and children, who made up the majority of the fort's inhabitants, quickly worked to turn their pewter spoons and plates into bullets. It made little difference.

On the morning of July 29, the settlers realized that they were surrounded by more than 300 well-armed British and Indian soldiers. Defeat was inevitable, so they negotiated a surrender. The women and children were allowed to leave the fort and make their way to Fort Augusta, in Sunbury. One desperate woman dressed her sixteen-year-old son in a dress to sneak him out with the women.

The fort's men were taken as captives to a nearby Indian encampment. There, under the supervision and participation of Hiokatoo, a notoriously brutal Iroquois, the men tomahawked and scalped each wounded American as the men pleaded for mercy. The surviving men were then placed under the protection of the British soldiers, who marched them long miles to Fort Niagara in Quebec, Canada. It was several years before any of the men were able to return home.

After the fort was surrendered, some thirty American soldiers gave chase to the British troops, but they were soon surrounded and routed. Half of the force was killed and scalped. Fort Freeland was burned.

The loss of Fort Freeland was devastating to the settlers. It left Fort Augusta open to attack with little warning. Few strongholds remained for some time on the frontier of Pennsylvania.

The Fort Today

The fort was not rebuilt after being burned in 1779. In 1829, the Hower-Slote House, a federal-style farmhouse, was built on the site. The spring that fed the fort is still visible. Local historical enthusiasts host Fort Freeland Day each year, complete with reenactments and history exhibits.

Directions

The Hower-Slote House now stands on the site of Fort Freeland. From I-180, just north of Route 80, take Exit 1. Head northeast on the Susquehanna Trail Road. Turn right on Warrior Run Boulevard, and then make a right into the parking area of the Hower-Slote House.

NEW NORWAY

Ole, Oleanna, Ole, Oleanna,
Oh, to be in Oleanna
That's where I'd like to be
Than to be in Norway
And bear the chains of slavery.
When I get to Oleanna,
That's where I'll settle down
In Oleanna the land is free
And money trees grow all around.

—TRANSLATED FROM DITMAR MEIDELL

History

The brilliant Norwegian violinist Ole (pronounced Oh'-lay) Borne-
man Bull founded New Norway in Potter County in 1853, with the
intention of creating a utopian society for Norwegian immigrants.
Bull fell in love with the beauty and promise of America while
touring the United States and Canada in the 1840s. He became enam-
ored of the warmth of the American people, the richness of the land,
and the prosperity that he saw all around him.

Bull had been a longtime political activist in Norway before coming to the United States. At that time, Sweden continued to claim sov-
ereignty over Norway, and young Norwegians chafed at losing their
culture and identity. Bull participated in many demonstrations against
the Swedish government during his youth. He became passionately
dedicated to the preservation of Norwegian culture.

In 1849, Bull founded the National Theater in Bergen, Norway, in
an effort to revitalize the Norwegian culture and art movement. The
theater was the first to present plays in native Norwegian, rather than
Danish. His writer and stage manager was none other than Henrik
Ibsen, whose famous character Peer Gynt was rumored to have been
based on Ole Bull.

Bull purchased more than seventeen square miles of land along Kettle Creek in Potter County, Pennsylvania, in 1852, from a Williamsport
businessman named John Cowan. Unfortunately, Cowan reserved
most of the tillable land for himself, making the land sold to Bull of
somewhat questionable value in terms of its ability to sustain a community. Bull was unaware of the true nature of the land he had bought,
apparently believing that he owned the entire tract. His intent was to
build four communities on the land in which Norwegians could live
and flourish: Valhalla, New Norway, New Bergen, and Oleana (also
spelled Oleanna).

The first Norwegians arrived in September 1852. By October,
almost 150 settlers had arrived. The community at New Norway had
already begun building, and it contained twenty log cabins and a
school by the summer of 1853. The Norwegians struggled to clear the
land, unaccustomed to creating tillable land from dense forest. Instead

of chopping the trees down, they attempted to remove them, roots and all, from the soil. This was difficult and time-consuming. Valuable time was lost in tree removal, slowing down the progress of the community as a whole.

Oleana was founded on September 8, 1852. Its 300 townspeople made their living with lumbering and woodworking. A small hospital and hotel were built in Oleana.

Nearby was the Valhalla settlement, where Ole Bull built his "castle," Nordjenskald, a two-story cottage with a lovely view of the verdant landscape. Before the cottage was completed, however, Bull realized that he was in financial peril. He had spent much of his own money to bring the Norwegian settlers to Potter County and build their houses. Now he had little left for his own home. He left to do a musical tour, periodically sending his earnings back to the New Norway community.

Winter was very difficult for the Norwegian immigrants. Although their native country also experienced bitter cold and snow, the first winter in New Norway was miserable, with few amenities and creature comforts available to the immigrants. The snow made traveling the four miles to the nearest town almost impossible, although it was the only way to procure food and supplies.

In addition, Bull became aware that the deed Cowan had given him reserved much of the usable land, meaning that the Norwegians were allowed to build only on the rocky mountainsides. Unfortunately, much of the building that had already occurred was on land owned by Cowan, including the hospital.

Realizing that economically, his venture was doomed to fail, Ole Bull sold his unfinished "castle" to Dr. Joerg, a German who had come to live in the colony. Joerg dismantled the cottage and built his own house on the eastern side of Kettle Creek, just south of where Bull's home had stood. In 1923, the house was destroyed by fire. The commonwealth of Pennsylvania established Ole Bull State Park on the land in 1920 and built the forest foreman's residence on the house site in 1929, which still stands.

Ole Bull returned to Norway, defeated by his failure at New Norway. He died of cancer in 1880 and was buried in his hometown of Bergen.

The Town Today

The commonwealth of Pennsylvania manages the land within Ole Bull State Park through the Pennsylvania Department of Conservation and Natural Resources. The site of Bull's "castle" can be viewed, as can the colony's cemetery. The people of Norway paid for the erection of a statue to honor Ole Bull in 2002. Little else remains of the utopian society.

Many of the facilities at the park were constructed during the Great Depression by the Civilian Conservation Corps (CCC). Hiking, swimming, camping, and picnics are all excellent summertime activities at New Norway today.

Directions

Ole Bull State Park lies on Route 144, 18 miles south of Galeton and 26 miles north of Renovo.

HICKS RUN

Founded more recently than many of the other Pennsylvania ghost towns, Hicks Run, in Cameron County, is yet another lumber town that used its raw materials faster than they could be renewed.

History

Hicks Run was founded in 1904 on the borders of Cameron and Elk Counties, in part by John E. DuBois, who also founded the much larger nearby town of Dubois. Hicks Run functioned as a lumber town for only eight years, until the forests had been depleted. When planned, it had been expected to last twice that long. Simple economics played a key role in the shortened lifespan of Hicks Run.

Two years after the sawmill was built and was busily turning out lumber and bark for tanning, Cameron County abruptly doubled the property taxes. In response, DuBois ordered the mill's output increased, doubling the number of shifts working, in an effort to increase the profit margin in the face of the greater tax load. Unfortunately, by doubling the shifts, DuBois concurrently doubled the rate of depletion of the forests surrounding the towns, thereby sealing the fate of Hicks Run.

Adding the second shift at the sawmill caused other problems as well. The night-shift workers argued that they should be paid more than those on the day shift. After tense negotiations and threats of being fired, they were given a 10 percent raise over the day-shift employees.

Most of the lumber for the mills was cut by a colorful group of workers known as wood hicks, who lived in various camps scattered throughout the forests around Hicks Run. The larger camps housed up to 200 men and consisted of semipermanent structures, including dormitories.

Compared with the living conditions of many Pennsylvania wood hicks, the Hicks Run camps were posh. Telephone service linked the camps to one another and the outside world. The dorms sported iron beds with mattresses, hot and cold running water, steam heating, and shower facilities. The grungy, smelly persona of the traditional wood hick was not considered acceptable in Hicks Run. Upon arriving at a camp, a new employee was ordered to shower. His clothing was taken from him and boiled. The greenhorn was given a temporary bed in an outbuilding. After a week, if the worker remained lice-free and relatively clean, he was allowed to take a bed in the regular dorm.

Most lumber operations avoided taking on the responsibilities of large camps such as those seen at Hicks Run. Several large operations maintained shacks for their workers and then burned them at the end of the work season, rebuilding them again in the spring. Hicks Run's accommodations likely seemed luxurious to many of the workers, and their cleanliness and sturdiness made them appropriate for keeping from year to year, rather than destroying them.

Although the wood hicks often descended upon the town to spend their paychecks partying, within the camps themselves life was regimented and orderly. The men had to be in bed with the lights out by 9 P.M. Alcohol was strictly forbidden in every camp. Violators were subject to termination and expulsion.

In many lumber camps, hostilities among ethnic groups was a frequent issue. Hicks Run was no exception. Though the Italian workers and native Pennsylvanians appeared to get along well, the Austrian immigrants who arrived to work in the lumbermill and the forests had much more difficulty assimilating. It was recognized that the Austrians were expert loggers, given their experiences in the alpine forests of their own country. In addition, they brought new technology and techniques for use in the Pennsylvania forests. But they were paid 10 cents an hour less than the Italian and American workers, which caused dissension and resentment. They ate their meals at a table separate from the others. Occasionally a group fight broke out between the Austrians and Pennsylvanians, but no significant injuries were reported.

Workers raved about the sumptuous meals prepared for them at the Hicks Run camps. Often a choice of meats was available, as were delicious pastries and snacks. This was unheard of at other wood hick camps. Reportedly, the cooks at one Hicks Run camp baked more than 12,000 pies in less than a year. It wasn't all a lark for the workers, though. The wood hicks were forbidden to talk at the table and were reprimanded by the cooks if they did so. It was surely a small price to pay for such delicious fare.

Oddly, the tenant houses in town were much more sparse and shabby than the wood hick camps in the forests. The tenant homes were given to the workers in an unpainted condition. Outhouses stood in the backyard of each house, and no electricity was available. There was running water in the homes, however. Lacking other alternatives, the tenants often papered their walls with newspapers, which served as a type of insulation. Kerosene lamps provided light, and coal and wood stoves heated the homes in winter. It made for rough living.

The area around Hicks Run was a sportsman's paradise. Enormous brook trout were frequently caught in the stream, as were eels, which were a gastronomic delicacy. Although deer were not plentiful in the area, bear hunting was popular.

Unfortunately, as with any lumber business, occasional tragedies were a part of life in Hicks Run. The first fatality occurred on March 9, 1906, when John Condon was crushed between two log cars on the railroad.

Shockingly, the other three fatalities at Hicks Run occurred within a few months of each other just as the town was dying out on its own. B. Segutia, an Italian railroad worker, attempted to climb onto a moving train and misstepped. He died en route to the Dubois hospital on the train that had severed his leg. The next victim was Charles Starr, who was killed by a log train while trying to throw a switch ahead of the car. He is buried in an unmarked grave at the feet of John Condon.

The third to be killed was Frank Laybarger, who was a strong proponent of vigilance in the workplace. Less than two hours before his death, he had given a stern speech to some lumber workers on the importance of being careful at all times when working around railroad cars. He showed the men his two missing fingers as an added caution. Shortly after, while crawling along some logs on a railroad car trying to set the brakes, he lost his balance, falling between the cars. He was crushed by the train. He is buried in the Hicks Run Cemetery, although his death was two days earlier than shown on the stone.

The Town Today

Today Hicks Run lies within the Pennsylvania State Game Lands and the Elk State Forest. Only a cemetery remains to mark what was once a bustling, successful lumber town. An elk observation deck stands above part of the former town site. Every evening at dusk, the elk arrive to delight the audiences who watch.

Directions

The site of Hicks Run lies just north of Route 555 in Cameron County. Coming from Elk County, take Route 555 east into Cameron County. About 1 mile over the Cameron County line, take a left on Houston Mill Road. Then take the first right. Hicks Run is 50 yards past the turn from Houston Mill Road.

AUSTIN

Although a town currently sits on the Austin site in Potter County, it is not the same town that was drowned in the dam burst of 1911.

History

The Austin lumbermill was built in 1886 by A. G. Lyman. A planing mill and kiln for drying lumber were erected nearby. As with all lumber operations, the threat of fire was a constant concern. In 1889, fire destroyed the Austin mill. It was rebuilt, but several fires over the years took their toll on the operation.

On September 30, 1911, the Austin Dam burst, demolishing the Goodyear mill upstream from Austin as a wall of water raced down through the valley. The lumber and logs from the destroyed mill were carried in a deadly wave down the river. The noise generated by the devastated mill as it churned in the floodwaters was deafening.

The managers of the Austin mill received a telephone call warning that the dam had burst. They rushed to evacuate the mill, calling to the workers at the kiln, planing mill, and lumbermill. The managers stopped to grab the mill's records from the safe as the workers fled, running for high ground.

They had not gone far when a horrific roaring sound reached their ears. The men turned and saw the wave of water with the hemlock logs from the Goodyear mill rushing toward them. The Austin men raced to safety. The mill managers believed that the presence of the Goodyear lumber was the only reason the Austin mill was not totally destroyed, as it essentially landed in the Austin millpond and served to break the force of the rushing floodwaters. The mill was heavily damaged, however, as was the rest of the town.

In all, seventy-nine official deaths were recorded, but many others likely were carried away. As some of the workers and residents of the area were not clearly documented, it is unclear how many truly perished in the flood. Many bodies were never recovered.

The Town Today

Today the modern town of Austin stands on and near the site of the earlier lumber town. The Austin School now stands where the mill once turned out quality lumber. The remains of the dam are still visible, a chilling reminder of the disaster that destroyed the town.

Directions

Austin is located along Route 872 in Potter County, southeast of Keating Summit.

Northeastern Pennsylvania

RICKETTS

The busy lumber town of Ricketts once thrived in the scenic mountains of Sullivan County.

History

Ricketts was founded in 1891 in a beautiful stretch of Sullivan County, southeast of Lopez. Col. Robert Ricketts, a decorated Civil War veteran, owned an enormous stretch of land in the area, consisting of more than 100 square miles in the mountains of north-central Pennsylvania. Colonel Ricketts hired Trexler and Turrell to cut the lumber on his land. The Trexler and Turrell Lumber Company then built a large sawmill in a flat area, as well as a pond to hold the logs.

The Ricketts family built a beautiful home on Ganoga Lake, about four miles southwest of the location of the town of Ricketts. It functioned as a hotel from 1873 to 1903, and then became the summer home of the family.

The actual village of Ricketts straddled the Sullivan and Wyoming County lines. On the Sullivan County side of town stood the sawmill and many of the homes in Ricketts. The town's hotel, store, and a stave mill were on the Wyoming County side.

Ricketts was a bustling place during its lifetime. It had two churches, Lutheran and Catholic. It also had a one-room and a two-room school.

The workers in Ricketts were vividly aware that they lived in a company town. Although they were paid in American currency (unlike workers in some other company towns, who received company currency in its stead), they were allowed to buy their merchandise only from the company store. The prices at the company store were inflated, and all purchases were on a credit basis. At the end of each month, the worker's tab was compared to his income, and he was paid the difference. Often the worker was left with less than $10 in income after settling his tab.

Several Ricketts workers realized that a store in nearby New Albany would fill their order for them. The men sent a rather large order and received their goods at considerable savings. But the Trexler and Turrell managers found out what the men had done and called them in for a stern meeting. The men were told in no uncertain terms that purchasing goods from outside stores again would result in their termination from their jobs.

Alcohol was forbidden in Ricketts. In order to have a drink, residents had to travel to Lopez, several miles north. One day a salesman from Lopez drove his wagon to Ricketts, intent on selling goods to the locals. He had several kegs of beer on the back of his wagon. While some men distracted the driver, others stole the kegs and rolled them down the hill to the town, hiding them until that evening. Several of the lumber workers had a wild party that night, but they were informed the next morning that they no longer were employed by Trexler and Turrell.

For entertainment, the people of Ricketts enjoyed simple pleasures such as their baseball team and the local band. Occasionally the locals took a train to Harvey's Lake for a town picnic or had square dances.

The residents of Ricketts paid $2.50 a month to rent their homes. The houses did not have electricity or running water. Many of the homes had four rooms total, with a kitchen and living area downstairs and two bedrooms upstairs. The houses were not well insulated and tended to be very cold in winter. To try to keep warm, the families often glued paper, including newspaper, onto the walls. To obtain water, women often carried buckets of water from wells around the town.

Health insurance in Ricketts had some similarity to today's plans. Workers paid $1 from each paycheck for health care, which was provided by Dr. Kingsley. The doctor provided not only medical services, but dental care as well. Dr. Kingsley is remembered for his disdain of chloroform, which was then a readily used sedative during dental procedures. Instead, he appeared to appreciate the challenge of finding two or three burly men from the street to hold down the frightened dental patient as the good doctor approached him or her with the pliers.

The mill at Ricketts was a busy place. A second band saw was added in 1898, several years after the mill was built, dramatically increasing its output. At its peak, lumber was cut at a rate of 300,000 board feet per day. By 1910, however, the depletion of the forests had diminished the output of the mill to 80,000 board feet per day. In a few short years, the former forest land was essentially bare. In 1914, the mill shut down, and the workers moved away.

The Town Today

The site of the former town of Ricketts is best visited before vegetation has a chance to grow, preferably in early spring. By summer, thick meadow grass and cattails obliterate any visible remnants of Ricketts. Visitors have reported that many foundations remain to this day.

Directions

The Ricketts site lies 4.5 miles north of the Ricketts Glen State Park entrance on Route 487, just below a parking area used by those hunting in the state game lands. The area has many snakes. Wear sturdy boots.

AZILUM

> High above the winding river,
> In a flood of morning sunlight,
> Near the Lodge of Rock Mount Summit,
> Oft I pause, of time forgetful,
> As I gaze across Asylum,—
> Rock-bound vale of dreams pathetic . . .
>
> —ELIZA ARNOUT

History

Azilum, one of the better-preserved ghost towns in Pennsylvania, is located on the Susquehanna River in Bradford County, near Towanda. The site was set aside by Robert Morris and others to serve as a refuge for aristocrats fleeing the French Revolution, as well as slave uprisings in Santo Domingo (now Haiti). The town was inhabited for only ten years, from 1793 to 1803. When Napoleon took power in France, he granted amnesty to all aristocratic refugees who wished to return, and in most cases, he gave them back their land. Although most families returned to France or Santo Domingo, a few remained behind and became some of Pennsylvania's more influential citizens.

The American Revolution had taken place not long before the foundation of Azilum. In some ways, it could be argued that the French support of America in the war against England was a catalyst for the French Revolution. General Lafayette, a prominent French citizen, had joined George Washington as a military hero and had also inspired his countrymen to support America's dream of independence and self-actualization. But the financial support from France, coupled with a crippling famine, dragged the French economy into ruin. The starving lower classes rose up against the aristocracy and royalty, frequently executing them during riots. The French aristocracy fled France in large numbers to other European sites, Santo Domingo, or America.

The aristocrats arriving in Philadelphia were met by American citizens who had previously emigrated from France, as well as other American supporters. The city continued to have great respect and admiration for the Marquis de Lafayette and wanted to make his countrymen feel at home in their place of exile. The Americans provided the French with lodging, board, and assistance in finding more permanent living arrangements.

The French were discontented in Philadelphia, however. Accustomed to formality, courtly behavior, and rigid manners, they found the Americans to be rather uncivilized and unrefined. Plans were made to develop a French town named Azilum in Bradford County so that the exiles would be more comfortable, and 100,000 acres were purchased, of which 300 were set aside for the town.

The first exiles arrived in Azilum on October 29, 1793, guided by Marquis Omer Talon, the governor of the new town. Their arrival in the fall proved to be somewhat problematic. Winter arrived early, and the pampered aristocrats were stranded in the wilderness with no shelter or infrastructure in the bitter cold. The local American settlers pitched in, helping the exiles hastily build log cabins and providing them with rations to keep them alive over the winter. Despite this assistance, the lifestyle was a rude shock to the artistocratic French refugees. For guidance, they looked toward their charismatic fellow exile Omer Talon.

Talon was a trusted, effective leader. He believed in leading not only with words, but also by example. With his tireless work and encouragement, the exiles survived the winter and began to work to establish a true town at Azilum as more refugees arrived.

The streets of Azilum were very wide, most being 60 feet across. Broad Street was an astounding 100 feet wide and ran in an east-west direction, terminating at the Susquehanna River, where the ferry dock stood. Just north of Broad Street, the residents had built a wharf for docking supply boats from Wilkes-Barre.

Lots were generally two-fifths of an acre, although some larger ones were available. In all, the town contained 420 lots. The homes were mostly log structures, partly because of the abundance of timber in the area, but also because of the haste required in building the cabins and houses. At its height, Azilum had some fifty homes, shops, a church, bakery, inn, blacksmith shop, and distillery. It was a busy, cohesive community.

One of the more distinctive structures in Azilum was the Great House, or King's House. It stood on Lot 418, in the northeastern quadrant of the town. It was a large, two-story home, measuring eighty by sixty feet. Historical reports suggest that it was the largest log home in America.

Another notable structure, the Queen's House, reportedly was built in the vain hope that Queen Marie Antoinette would emigrate to Azilum and live there. But she was captured and beheaded before she could flee France. The site of the Queen's House has been the subject of some dispute. Many accounts place it approximately eight miles southwest of Azilum. It supposedly stood near a bakery and servants' homes. Charles Homet, supervisor of building construction in Azilum, had stained-glass windows installed in the home, which was intended to be grand and beautiful. Homet, having worked in the royal household, was well qualified to anticipate the creature needs of a queen in exile.

Azilum's governor, Marquis Omer Talon, had been forced into exile in France, where his arrest and execution had been ordered. While waiting for a ship to take him to safety in America, Talon met a young man at the port, Bartholemew LaPorte. The two men struck up a friendship, and Talon offered the job of valet to LaPorte, which he accepted. Shortly before departing for America, Talon learned that his arrest was imminent. LaPorte helped Talon squeeze into an empty wine cask, which was then loaded onto the ship. Once safely under way, LaPorte freed his employer from the barrel.

By all accounts, LaPorte was a loyal, hardworking employee. He became trusted with increasing responsibility and was promoted several times. He married Elizabeth Franklin in 1797, and their son John was born in the King's House in Azilum in 1798.

Another Azilum resident, Baron Charles Felix Bue Boulogne, came to America with Lafayette and fought the British alongside the American militia. He fell in love with America and made it his home. He became a land agent, obtaining large tracts of land for French exiles, and traveled back to France to invite the beleaguered aristocracy to join him in America and make Azilum their new home. Boulogne later drowned near Hillsgrove while trying to cross the Loyalsock Creek and became the first white person to be buried in Sullivan County. He is interred in an unmarked grave in the cemetery beside the Hillsgrove Methodist Episcopal Church.

Two sisters from a wealthy French family, Madame d'Autremont and Madame LeFevre, fled with their families to Philadelphia in 1792. They each purchased 300 acres in New York from Boulogne. By the time the families had traveled through the endless forests to arrive at their new lands, it was approaching winter, and it was impossible to do much more than build a rough shelter to sustain them through the long, bitter cold season.

The d'Autremonts and LeFevres had been accustomed to a life of luxury in France and had never endured such hardship or brutal weather. The nearby Indians were friendly and supplied the settlers with meat and other provisions, which enabled them to survive the winter. The Azilum settlers heard news of the families' plight and set out to retrieve them. They brought the beleaguered group to Azilum, where they remained.

Charles Homet was another significant resident of Azilum. An employee of the king of France at the time of the revolution, Homet narrowly escaped when the king was arrested. He made his way to the Bay of Biscay to wait for an American ship. When it arrived in port, he quietly placed his belongings on the boat and hid overnight onshore with friends. As the new day dawned, Homet realized that his pursuers had found him. He raced for the ship, only to find that it was moored five miles out at sea. Homet did not hesitate. He dove into the water and swam the entire distance to the ship.

Another passenger on Homet's ship was the lovely Marie Shillenger, a German who had been a lady-in-waiting to Marie Antoinette, but with the revolution had been forced to flee. The two fell in love on their journey to America and were married shortly after arriving in Philadelphia. They traveled to Azilum in 1794, where they lived in the Queen's House for two years.

Ten years after the foundation of Azilum, Napoleon took over as leader of France and set about unifying the splintered, war-torn country. One of his first actions was to invite the displaced aristocracy to return to France, with the promise of restoring to them their homes and land. When the exiles in Azilum received word of Napoleon's offer, they celebrated wildly, shouting "Viva la France!" Most gave little thought to remaining in the country that had opened its doors to them in a time of need. They celebrated for several days and then began packing to return to France.

> Peace restored, and warfare ended,
> Many Frenchmen left Asylum.
> Sailed away, with hearts o'erflowing,
> Sought their homes, and native country.
> Thus the village was deserted,
> Save a few who loved Asylum,
> Loved the sheltered little valley,
> Made their homes, and cast their future
> With America, the Free Land,
> With their new adopted country.
>
> —ELIZA ARNOUT

Only three of the forty French families remained in their new homeland after their neighbors returned to France: the Homets, LeFevres, and LaPortes. Charles Homet purchased the southern part of the valley for his family. His sons later founded a town across the river named Homets Ferry.

The LeFevre family moved across the river to Lime Hill and built the Inn on Lime Hill, which was renowned for its excellent food. The steaks attracted visitors from far and wide, who made their way to the LeFevres' inn.

Bartholemew LaPorte purchased the northern portion of the valley and lived in the King's House until his death. His son John built the LaPorte House, a beautiful mansion that served as a summer home, on the Azilum plot in 1836, long after the town had been deserted. John had the Queen's House torn down shortly thereafter as a potential fire hazard. John LaPorte was an active politician and businessman, holding many offices, including U.S. congressman, associate judge of courts in Bradford County, and state surveyor general. The lovely town of LaPorte, the Sullivan County seat, was named for Judge John LaPorte.

After the exodus, almost all structures were destroyed or removed from Azilum. In recent years, however, a nonprofit group called French Azilum, Inc., located a few of the cabins in nearby towns, where they were being used as sheds and outbuildings. The cabins have since been returned to the Azilum site.

The Town Today

Azilum has been partially restored by French Azilum, Inc., and a few of the original cabins and the LaPorte House are open for tours. The site is open to the public weekends in spring and Wednesday through Sunday in summer and fall. It is closed in winter. A nominal admission fee is charged.

A gift shop is housed in one of the cabins. Another is used for showing guests an informative video about Azilum and displaying some artifacts from the era. Walking trails meander through the grounds and pass by a beautiful stretch of the Susquehanna River. The remains of a wine cellar are clearly visible.

The LaPorte House still stands intact, and you can take a guided tour of the home. Although many of the items inside are not original, the house itself is impressive and showcases architecture and antiques appropriate to the era. While touring the LaPorte House, be vigilant for the ghosts who supposedly reside there. Both staff and visitors have reported seeing several benign spirits: young girls in clothing from the 1800s darting across doorways and a teenage girl in period dress ascending the staircase.

Directions

To reach Azilum, travel east to Wysox on U.S. Route 6. Turn south on Route 187. Turn east on SR 2014 and proceed for 3.5 miles to Azilum. Signs are posted along the way.

CELESTIA

The community of Celestia was situated in Sullivan County, one of the more beautiful places in Pennsylvania. It serves as an example of great religious devotion and disillusionment, as well as the financial realities that plague Americans even today.

History

Peter Armstrong, a Millerite, laid out Celestia in 1850 on a purchase of slightly more than 600 acres. Millerites were followers of William Miller, a religious leader who preached that Christ would return to earth on October 22, 1844. Miller was born a Baptist in 1782 and grew up in rural New York State. After serving as a soldier in the War of 1812, he suffered a crisis of faith and began to study the Bible in an attempt to reconcile the inconsistencies in his life and beliefs.

When Miller read Daniel 8:14, he was inspired. The verse discusses a 2,300-day prophecy. Most Christians viewed the passage as a description of a cleansing of the world by fire to make way for the second coming of Christ. Miller became convinced that the date referred to was October 22, 1844. By the time that date arrived, the Millerite movement had more than 100,000 followers, who consisted of Baptists, Presbyterians, Congregationalists, and Methodists.

The date that Miller believed would mark the coming of the Messiah came and went. This became known as the Great Disappointment, and thousands left the Millerite movement. The remaining followers struggled to understand where the prophecy had gone wrong. One, Joseph Bates, decided that the sanctuary Daniel 8:14 referred to as being cleansed actually resided in heaven, not on earth. He published a pamphlet espousing this "seventh day doctrine," which inspired James and Ellen White to accept this belief. The Whites and Joseph Bates became prominent leaders in the formation of the Seventh Day Adventist Church.

Many of Miller's followers continued to believe in the imminent return of the Son of God here on earth. Peter Armstrong and his followers trusted the literal interpretation of the Bible as set forth by

Miller. The prophet Isaiah commanded, "In the wilderness prepare ye the way of the Lord," so they set about to live in the wilderness and wait for the Messiah's coming. Armstrong felt that his calling in life was to prepare the way for Christ and build a utopian, communistic society that was a perfect theocracy. He laid out the town of Celestia in Sullivan County in 20-by-100-foot lots, which he sold to the faithful. By 1853, he had sold 300 such plots at $10 each.

By 1860, the town included homes, a store, meetinghouse, sawmill, and related outbuildings. With the start of the American Civil War, the Celestians were convinced that the return of Christ was imminent. Surely the war was the embodiment of the fiery time of judgment that would precede the second coming. While excited by the apparent approach of the time of the second coming, Armstrong was concerned that the members of his settlement might be pressed into service in the Union Army to fight in the war. In an effort to prevent his followers from becoming embroiled in the conflict, Armstrong declared that the Celestians were "peaceable aliens and wilderness exiles from the rest of the Commonwealth of Pennsylvania" and should be exempt from the draft. They may have been the first examples of conscientious objectors in the country.

For the most part, Celestia was economically self-sufficient, with active farming as well as the sawmill and a machine shop. Additional income was gained from contributions from resident nonbelievers and the sale of wool and maple products. It was far from a wealthy settlement, but initially the community appeared to be a success.

In a gutsy move, Armstrong decided to deed a large portion of the community to God and Jesus for their use as they saw fit. In doing so, he believed that the land was no longer his and therefore no longer subject to the tax laws of the commonwealth. After all, how does one send a tax bill to God?

Sullivan County was not amused. In 1876, it found Armstrong in significant arrears for taxes. He was unable to pay and was forced to sell the property to his son, who attempted to pick up where his father had left off. But he lacked some of the charisma that had drawn followers to his father, and by 1878, the discouraging sale of the land and change in leadership had taken a toll on morale in Celestia.

Believers began to doubt the Millerite doctrines and moved away. Nonbelievers moved into the town in larger numbers, often in an attempt to avoid the draft, hide from society, or live comfortably at the expense of the community.

Dismayed by the secular nature of many of the newcomers to Celestia, Peter Armstrong founded a second village in 1872 named Glen Sharon, near Sonestown. The second village never fully realized its potential, and it rapidly declined along with Celestia.

Peter Armstrong died on June 20, 1887, in Celestia, at the age of sixty-nine. By that time, very few residents remained. The town eventually faded into the wild beauty of Sullivan County.

The Town Today

Though the town of Celestia no longer exists today, some foundations and the remains of a road can still be found at the site.

Directions

To access Celestia, a parking area is located 1.5 miles west of Laporte on Route 42. A historical marker makes it easy to find. You can obtain a self-guided tour brochure at the Sullivan County Historical Society Museum in Laporte.

LAQUIN

It is difficult to believe that large communities can simply disappear. Looking at photos of Laquin at its height, it is impossible to think that few traces remain of this bustling Bradford County community of hardworking Pennsylvanians.

History

Laquin earned prominence in the early 1900s as the second-largest manufacturing community in Bradford County. At its most productive, 1,000 people were employed at the town's Schrader lumbermill, which was built in 1902, along with many of the homes in Laquin, and began milling operations in April 1903. The mill was enormous, with a total footprint of 161 by 330 feet. The mill processed 125,000 to 150,000 board feet of lumber each day.

The lumber company was owned by the Union Tanning Company. The leather-tanning business needed the hemlock bark found in huge amounts in the surrounding forest. The tract of land surrounding the Schrader Mill in Laquin was estimated to contain half a billion board feet of lumber.

Early on, there were plans for an array of factories: a chemical plant to manufacture acetate, a kindling wood factory, a cooperage to make barrel staves, and a factory to make wagon wheel hubs and wood chips for brewing beer. The growing workforce in Laquin swelled the town, turning it into a large industrial and residential community. At its peak, it was a sprawling, bustling village. As one entered the town and passed the chemical factory, enormous rows of drying wood greeted the eye. Just past the stave factory stood ten double houses in which workers lived. Behind the stave sheds was the hub plant.

Beyond the row homes was a popular baseball field, as well as the Schrader sawmill. The kindling factory stood near the sawmill. On the north side of town stood a school, a Methodist and a Baptist church, and the majority of homes for the employees of the sawmill and railroad. Both churches were well attended and held morning and evening services. There was a refreshing spirit of cooperation between denominations. At times, one church or the other would be temporarily without a minister, and the other would always open its doors to the congregants.

Although most of the 110 single- and double-family homes in Laquin were unpainted, they were relatively posh compared with those in many lumbering towns. Running water from springs was piped into all the houses. They had plastered walls, unlike many lumber-town homes, which used newspaper for insulation. Most had electricity, but they did not have central heating and were warmed by the kitchen stoves. It was not surprising for residents to wake up in winter with frost and snow covering the foot of the bed.

The town also had a company store, barbershop, hotel, post office, Odd Fellows Hall, and a railway station for the Susquehanna and New York Railroads. As the town grew, a small school was built, but it was outgrown even before construction was completed. A second two-story building was added to supplement the school space. Several of the school's female teachers actually lived several hours away, in Elmira, New York, and commuted home on weekends—no small task by rail.

There was no direct mail delivery in Laquin. Instead, the town post office was a common area where residents met, picked up mail, exchanged news, and caught up with one another. The town also enjoyed a restaurant and ice cream parlor, which served as busy meeting places for the locals. In later years, a billiard hall replaced the ice cream parlor.

The young people of Laquin were, in general, fun-loving and upstanding. Although they loved to dance and have fun together, they were, as a group, against the use of alcohol. Instead, they competed in candymaking competitions, sleigh riding, and square dances.

Laquin residents were also known for their skills in honey hunting. They put drops of anise into wooden boxes with sliding glass covers to attract bees. Once bees were caught, they took the boxes into the woods and opened them. The honey hunters then followed the bees until they led to trees containing honey.

The company store was lively while the mill was in operation. It employed seven clerks and two butchers. The second floor served as a furniture store. Claude Mapes ran the company store for years. He then became the postmaster during the years following the closing of the store and the mill, when Laquin became the location of a Civilian Conservation Corps (CCC) camp. He was the last resident of Laquin, finally moving away in 1941.

The Laquin Hotel was a boardinghouse for many of the unmarried employees in the area. For several years, it contained a bar serving alcohol to the townspeople as well as the residents of the hotel. During one of the mill's ownership changes, the bar was removed and alcohol use was actively discouraged. But where there is a will, there is a way, and some of the workers hastily erected stills in the woods around Laquin to provide liquor.

Though the sawmill and other businesses in Laquin had little difficulty attracting employees, some of the town's jobs were repugnant, and only impoverished immigrants could be persuaded to do them. One such job was that of pushing carts laden with wood in and out of the retorts, or drying rooms. The temperatures inside the retorts could reach 1,000 degrees Fahrenheit, making the work dangerous and unpleasant. One employee of such a job was unceremoniously informed that he had to work all day on Christmas or be fired. The man dutifully reported to work on Christmas, worked all day without complaint, and left work at the end of his shift. He then went on a bender, staying drunk and not appearing for work for more than a week. When he finally returned to the retort, his enraged supervisor threatened to fire him. The man calmly replied that no one had mentioned that he had to work on the days *after* Christmas. His boss relented, all too aware that the man would be very difficult to replace.

As in all lumber towns, work at the sawmill had inherent dangers, such as railroad accidents. In one devastating accident in 1907, a log car broke loose from an engine on a steep grade and plummeted back toward town, killing seven railway workers in the crash. The wreck was the worst log-train wreck in Pennsylvania history.

The Schrader sawmill was bought and sold, closed and reopened before finally closing down for good, ceasing production on August 6, 1925. This left only the chemical plant in operation to employ the townspeople. The town struggled briefly, and then died out.

The Town Today

If you can navigate the backroads of rural Pennsylvania, the actual site of the town of Laquin is easy to find. The current owners of the land have a large sign at the top of their driveway that proudly proclaims, "The Town of Laquin." It is strongly recommended that you check with the landowners before visiting their property. Besides the obvious common courtesy involved in obtaining permission to poke around, you should know that the current owners have several large dogs and a pet mountain lion.

Across the road from the property, 100 feet up a faint trail, you can find the ruins of the Laquin Hotel.

Many foundations, including the sawmill and several houses, are scattered around the current owner's property. The owners also display relics from the town in their garden, including the door to the sawmill's safe.

Directions

From Canton, in Bradford County, take Route 414 east. At East Canton, make a right onto SR 3005. Make the next left onto Southside Road, which runs parallel to Route 414. Turn right onto Mountain Road. When the road terminates at a T, turn right onto Laquin Road. Look for the sign marking the site of the former town.

CENTRALIA

No discussion of Pennsylvania ghost towns would be complete without Centralia, in Columbia County. With all due respect to the few intrepid souls who remain in their homes today, Centralia often looks like a vision of hell, with crumbling infrastructure, silent streets, and smoke and sulfurous fumes rising from numerous fissures in the ground throughout the area.

History

Centralia was initially populated by Indians, who sold the huge wilderness of northeastern Pennsylvania to Colonial agents in 1794 for $750. Stephen Girard, a banker from Philadelphia, purchased the land that included Centralia in 1830 for $39,000. In the region, he found a vein of anthracite coal.

The town that later became Centralia was initially named Bull's Head. The first building, erected in 1841, was called the Bull's Head Tavern. It was a log structure that stood until 1916. By 1860, the town was large enough to support its own post office. The townspeople decided that Bull's Head was a poor choice for a name, so they renamed the town Centerville. But when they tried to register the name for the post office, they learned that it was already taken. Centralia was then proposed and officially became the town's name.

Initially, the Centralia region itself was ignored by coal prospectors, despite the successful mining operations nearby. Alexander Rea, a mining engineer, is credited with finally exploiting Centralia's coal riches. Unfortunately, Rea was not able to enjoy the windfall that might have been his. He was brutally murdered by the Molly Maguires as he drove his buggy between Mount Carmel and Centralia. Rea's murderer, Patrick Hester, was arrested and then set free. He was later rearrested and tried for the murder ten years after the crime, when he was found guilty and hanged.

The Molly Maguires were a violent organization of Irish-Americans who often committed murder and arson under the auspices of furthering the cause of the rights of Irish miners. Though the Irish miners were indeed often oppressed by their English and Welsh supervisors, the retaliatory behavior of the Molly Maguires is largely viewed as criminal in modern times. Their reign of terror lasted from 1862 to 1877, when many of the group's leaders were hanged.

In 1948, the second-worst plane disaster to that date occurred just outside Centralia. Rescue efforts were based in town, where injured and dead passengers were brought. When one plane crash victim's body went unclaimed by his New York relatives, he was adopted by the kind people of Centralia. The town paid for his funeral and a plot in the Odd Fellows Cemetery, which was just adjacent to the site where the infamous mine fire later started. To this date, displaced citizens of Centralia still return to put flowers on the grave of a man who, though a total stranger, was important enough to remember.

The Centralia mine fire began on May 17, 1962, when the town council agreed to clean up the landfill by burning it. Members of the local volunteer fire company were on the scene to extinguish the blaze when the cleanup was complete. When the group was done burning the trash, the firemen poured water on the pile. No remaining flame was visible, so everyone left.

But unbeknownst to all, the fire was still smoldering. It continued to burn though the garbage dump, burning deeper and deeper, until it reached the vein of anthracite coal. On May 19, the flames again became visible from the nearby cemetery. The firemen returned and attempted to extinguish the fire, but it proved to be remarkably stubborn. After several days of trying to quench the fire, the firemen realized that there was a trench under the garbage dump that led to the anthracite mines.

Some suggest today that if workers had dug nonstop in the first days following the discovery of the fire, the mine fire might have been extinguished. Instead, work was paused in order to open it up to the bid process. By the time significant attempts to stop the fire's progress were made, it was too late.

As the mine fire slowly smoldered, the reality of the dangers posed to the town became apparent. Deadly gases were being created and began rising into citizens' basements and homes. The U.S. Office of Surface Mining placed large vent pipes around the town to release the gases safely. Even the mayor of Centralia was overcome by the noxious fumes in his home, leading to his hospitalization. Residents had alarms in their homes to warn them of dangerous levels of gases, but there were not enough working alarms to go around. Instead, those living near the clearly burning vein of coal had to borrow monitors from neighbors in safer areas.

The mine fire burned hotter than the planet Mercury, often reading 1,000 degrees Fahrenheit. The mines were subsequently completely uninhabitable by miners, and work ceased. The mines actually exacerbated the problem, as the mine shafts provided the fire with needed oxygen.

One of the more dramatic incidents in Centralia occurred on Valentine's Day 1981, when a twelve-year-old boy, Todd Domboski, stopped to inspect a plume of smoke rising from the ground. The ground beneath him abruptly gave way, and Todd found himself sunken into the earth up to his knees. As the terrified boy tried to scramble out, the earth separated again, dropping him out of sight. He screamed for help.

Although his head was only three feet below ground level, Todd continued to slide downward. He grabbed an exposed tree root to slow his descent. Odoriferous steam swirled around him, making it difficult to breathe or remain oriented. The fire below greedily sucked the air around him, creating a wind that whipped around him. A hand appeared from above just in time, and Todd grasped it gratefully. He was dragged to safety by his cousin Eric. Todd's close call proved to be a catalyst for some governmental agencies to address the issues in Centralia.

Almost twenty years after the start of the fire, the government estimated that the cost of extinguishing it would approach $660 million. Instead, it decided to institute a $50 million buyout of the town. Most of the townspeople left voluntarily during the buyout, but many stayed. The decision of whether to evacuate was an intensely emotional one for people whose families had been in the area for generations. Neighbors turned against neighbors, those who took the buyouts being viewed as traitors. Even among family members, the fight over whether to leave caused great distress.

In one particularly sad incident in the 1990s, a Centralia man informed his wife of his decision to evacuate. She refused to go. The argument between them escalated until the man resorted to physical violence and he murdered his wife. Overcome with shame and horror, the man drove into the mountains, poured gasoline over himself, and lit a match.

The government declared that the voluntary buyout was mandatory in the 1990s, under Governor Casey. Despite this, some residents refused to leave. More than a decade later, the government has not forcibly removed these people. The fire still burns to this day, and as it continues to do so, the slowly burning coal seam may begin to threaten other towns in the area, such as nearby Ashland.

The Town Today

The town of Centralia still stands, though in an altered form, today. Some note that it more closely resembles the community of 1841 than a modern village. The government has ceased services to the town, including postal service, mowing, and repair work. Many of the houses have been torn down, and others shuttered. Single slender houses remain from rows of houses, now supported by joists rather than by identical row homes.

Pipes used to vent the gas and steam poke through the ground in various places, and smoke curls lazily from their openings. In other spots, smoke rises from the ground, indicating the current position of the fire.

A few intrepid souls continue to live in Centralia. They dread the day that the state of Pennsylvania may decide to enforce the mandatory evacuation signed by Governor Casey. The remaining residents note that their town continues to sit on one of the largest veins of valuable anthracite coal that exists. They contend that the government plans to evict them from their homes in order to mine the coal and keep the profits. The remaining inhabitants are considered to be squatters, as the state now owns their homes and land. The government denies any plans to mine the coal found beneath the town.

In 1962, Centralia was home to more than 1,100 people. Now only about 10 remain.

Directions

Centralia is located just north of Ashland, along Route 61. Access to the town is not easy, and following detour signs will take you away from the area. If you approach by foot, use extreme caution. The ground is unsafe in spots and may be prone to collapse. In addition, the gases and smoke rising from the fire are considered unsafe. Visit Centralia only with caution and at your own risk.

ECKLEY

Luzerne County's Eckley today incorporates a little bit of Hollywood into the history of a coal patch town.

History

Following the discovery of a vein of valuable anthracite coal beneath the village of Shingleton, Sharpe, Leisenring, and Company purchased the rights to the coal. In 1854, it leased 1,500 acres of land from the wealthy family of Judge Charles Coxe of Philadelphia, who owned much of the land in the Hazleton area. Shingleton was named for the wooden shingles that had provided the main income for the local residents before the coal-mining operation.

Mining activities quickly began at what was named the Council Ridge Colliery. Housing for the workers was quickly built, and a small town boomed around the Shingleton area seemingly overnight. Besides the coal mine, a sawmill was erected to process raw timber from the enormous hemlock and pine forests of the area. Sharpe, Leisenring, and Company also built a large coal breaker, engine house, blacksmith shop, and oil house.

Although shingles continued to be manufactured and sold, it was evident that Shingleton was no longer an appropriate name for a town in which coal was king, and in 1857, the residents decided to change the name of the town. Initially they named the town Fillmore, after President Millard Fillmore. But when they applied for a post office, they were informed that another town named Fillmore already existed in Pennsylvania. The townspeople then decided to name the town Eckley, after Eckley B. Coxe, the son of the landowner Judge Coxe.

Eckley Coxe was an accomplished man in his own right. Besides controlling more than 35,000 acres of land with his family business, Coxe Brothers and Company, he also served in the Pennsylvania Senate. He later helped establish the American Institute of Mining Engineers and served as president of the American Society of Mechanical Engineers.

At its peak in 1870, Eckley had 1,500 residents. The town had two churches, a company store, hotel, butcher shop, shoe shop, doctor's office, tailor, and icehouse.

Social stratification was obvious in Eckley, which was separated into quarters. At the west end of the village, the handsome homes of the business owners were located. The home of Richard Sharpe, one of the company owners, was considered to be one grandest in the area. In the next quarter stood the homes of the managers and contractors. The other two quarters of town were inhabited by the miners and laborers.

The workers' homes were built to look similar to one another. Little attention was given to aesthetics or individuality. Because these paint pigments were the cheapest to buy, all houses were painted red with black trimwork. The interior walls were insulated with shredded newspaper.

Living conditions were typical of impoverished communities. The workers lived in squalor, for the most part, with reeking outhouses, filthy sewage ditches, and poor garbage removal. Indoor plumbing was finally installed in most homes starting in 1924, which provided some relief. Before that, residents had to carry water home from community pumps, which at times were contaminated from the untreated sewage leaching into the water supply. Illness was a constant threat in Eckley.

The grueling work of mining the anthracite was performed in shafts and tunnels by men wielding pickaxes and shovels. It was hazardous work, with cave-ins, explosions, and tunnel flooding posing constant threats to the miners. More insidious dangers lurked as well: Black lung, or miner's asthma, was caused by breathing in the coal dust. The afflicted miner would suffer from shortness of breath and inevitably face a miserable death. The coal miners provided an essential resource to the people of Pennsylvania, and America, for little pay and great hardship.

Before the days of child labor laws, young children worked alongside the men in the colliery. These young boys often started their coal-mining careers as breaker boys, watching the rocks come through the breaker chutes to the bottom. Their task was to pick out the rock and slate, leaving only the coal. After they reached age twelve, they would begin manning the mine tunnel doors. This important job helped regulate air flow in the tunnels. They were also responsible for stopping the coal cars by throwing hardwood clubs into the wheel spokes. By age fourteen, they became full-fledged miners.

Women were not exempt from the hard work of life in a patch town. They were responsible for washing clothes, ironing, baking, sewing and mending, and cleaning, all of which were difficult in a town with no plumbing or running water.

At its peak, Eckley produced nearly 125,000 tons of coal annually. Transporting the coal from the mines proved to be an expensive proposition. Just as it began to look as if the cost of mining in the area could not be overcome, and the Council Ridge Colliery was in danger of being shut down, the steamboat industry sprang onto the scene in America. Steamboats required huge amounts of coal to fuel them, and Eckley anthracite was widely viewed as the cleanest burning. The coal-mining industry in Eckley was rejuvenated, and the town rejoiced.

The start of the Civil War in 1861 also increased the demand for coal from Eckley, as the Union Navy demanded enormous amounts to supply its steamships. The famous ironclad ship the *Monitor* was burning Eckley coal during its battle with the Confederate *Merrimack* in March 1862.

Following the end of the Civil War, labor disputes and strikes dampened the relative prosperity that Eckley had enjoyed. The advent of strip mining in 1890, which required fewer miners to extract the coal from the earth, sealed Eckley's fate. By 1920, the population had dropped to fewer than 600 residents.

The greatly reduced mining operation was sold several times. By 1968, George Huss owned the land that had once belonged to the Coxe family and was doing some strip mining around Eckley. He was approached by Paramount Pictures, which was interested in filming the movie *The Molly Maguires* in the area. The studio executives were impressed by how authentic Eckley looked. Huss leased the entire village of Eckley for a year to Paramount Pictures while it filmed the movie. The film company built the enormous coal breaker now seen in the town, as well as other structures intended to look typical of the period.

In 1971, Huss sold Eckley to the Anthracite Historical Site Museum, which in turn deeded it to the commonwealth of Pennsylvania to be managed by the Pennsylvania Historical and Museum Committee.

The Town Today

Today Eckley Miners' Village is open to visitors year-round, with two dozen restored buildings that you can tour for an admission fee. A walking tour is clearly marked throughout the village, and guided tours can also be arranged.

The visitors center stands across the street from the Church of Immaculate Conception, which is the start of the walking tour of Eckley. The church was built in 1861 to serve the town's Irish Catholic residents. The tour includes residences that stood at the time of the town, as well as other structures built more recently by the movie studio: a mule barn, company store, and the coal breaker. Picnic facilities are available.

Directions

To reach Eckley, take I-80 to the White Haven exit. Turn left onto Route 940 and go 6 miles to Freeland. Turn right onto Highland Road and follow the signs to the Eckley Miners' Village.

Southwestern Pennsylvania

BEELOR'S FORT

Beelor's Fort, a frontier fort in Washington County, doubled as a maternity ward.

History

In 1774, Cap. Sam Beelor obtained the rights to 400 acres west of Pittsburgh, which he named Big Levels, for some inexplicable reason. His son Sam Jr. also bought land nearby. Soon after, Alexander Dunlap and his son John bought adjoining property. The men quickly began building Beelor's Fort.

The two-story fort was intended to protect the four men's families from hostile Indians. It was a formidable structure, with a stockade fence around it. Records show that the fort served as a meeting place as well as a makeshift church for religious services. Several additional families moved into the area and also used the fort for protection and community activities.

In September 1779, Sam Brady and his Rangers trailed a raiding party of fourteen Wyandot Indians who appeared to be headed for Beelor's Fort. Brady and his team prepared an ambush to meet the war party as it returned. The Indians had spent two hours attacking Beelor's Fort, succeeding in killing four settlers and capturing three men. Brady's group killed most of the Indians and safely rescued the captured men.

Apparently Beelor's Fort served as the local maternity ward as well. In 1790, Timothy and Hannah Shane outran an Indian war party, making it safely to the fort. The Indians attacked, and as the battle raged on, Hannah gave birth to a son, John. Similarly, Martha McDonald was pregnant with twins when she was told that Indians were approaching. She clambered onto a horse and rode the five bumpy miles to Beelor's Fort just ahead of the raiding Indians. Shortly thereafter, she safely gave birth to William and Andrew.

Not all stories of Beelor's Fort ended so happily. In 1790, five local men gathered to harvest wheat near the fort. One, William Bailey, sat on a stump to rest while the others walked to a creek to get a drink of the cool water. Indians attacked, killing the four men at the creek. They captured Bailey when he slipped in mud while fleeing and started toward the Ohio River with their captive.

Somehow, word of the raid reached the fort, where a group quickly assembled to rescue their friend. The rescuers reached the Ohio River just as the Indians launched their canoes, one of which held a bound William Bailey. The settlers shot at the Indians, killing several, including the warrior paddling Bailey's canoe. The Indian toppled over, capsizing the canoe and dumping Bailey into the fast-moving river. The rescue team sprang into action, swimming to a struggling Bailey and dragging him to shore.

The Fort Today

The fort's site is located in the village of Candor, in Washington County, about five miles east of Burgettstown and three miles north of Midway. Little remains of the actual fort today.

Directions

From U.S. Route 22 west, drive to SR 980, also named McDonald-Midway Road. Take SR 980 south 1.8 miles to Beech Hollow Road and turn right on Beech Hollow Road. At Candor Road, make a left. Proceed south .4 mile on Candor Road to the Raccoon Presbyterian Church. On a plateau of land 100 yards southwest of the church stands a small house on the site of Beelor's Fort.

OLD ECONOMY VILLAGE

The experimental community of Old Economy Village, in Beaver County, was a resounding success for more than fifty years.

History

In 1785, a young German named George Rapp was seized with a religious vision. He felt called to break from the Lutheran Church and try to interpret the Bible more literally. He soon began his own movement, in which he and his followers sought perfect harmony within themselves. These Harmonists followed the book of Revelations, which stated, "into the wilderness . . . for a time and times, and half a time."

Rapp and 600 of his followers moved from Germany to the wilds of Pennsylvania in 1804 in an effort to fulfill the words of Revelations to move to the wilderness to wait for the coming of the next Messiah. The group bought a 9,000-acre tract of land in Butler County in which to establish their Harmony Society.

The society was communistic, believing that all property was held for the common good and not individually owned. This belief was consistent with the beliefs of the early Christian church. After three years, the Harmonists also adopted celibacy, believing that they were preparing themselves "solely for Christ and His Kingdom."

Procreation was not an issue for the Harmonists, who believed that the return of Christ was imminent. They were convinced that the

Messiah would return to earth in 1829, ending the world as it currently existed and making reproduction of Harmonist members completely unnecessary. The goal of the group was to travel with Christ to Jerusalem to build the temple there.

Initially the group survived by farming and crafts. By 1814, however, emphasis had shifted to manufacturing. The Harmonists sold their own domestic cotton, wool, and linen at market. Their society was self-sufficient, although they did continue to purchase some items from the outside world.

In 1814, the Harmonists left Pennsylvania and moved to Indiana, where they remained for another decade. They returned to Pennsylvania in 1824 to build their final home, settling on 3,000 acres along the Ohio River. Although the first two settlements had been named Harmony and New Harmony, this third village was named Oekonomie, which was Greek for Divine Economy. The 600 Harmonists in the village thought this name was appropriate because they believed that perfection in life and faith was accomplished through the appropriate use of time, materials, and hard work.

Within a year and a half, the Harmonists had constructed their town. The 200 buildings in the settlement were well built in comparison with others in the region. Many were made with bricks and other durable materials, rather than more degradable materials such as wood.

The village was a prosperous one. The Harmony Society was a major stockholder for some time in the Pittsburgh and Lake Erie Railroad. The Harmonists eventually sold their shares to Cornelius Vanderbilt in 1892. This, coupled with other shrewd investments and industry, created a very wealthy community with little of the deprivation and wistfulness seen in other experimental communistic societies.

Besides the textile manufacturing, which provided economic stability for the village, Rapp also began to make wine for retail sale. Their wine was much sought after throughout Pennsylvania.

In a vault below George Rapp's house, the society stored almost half a million dollars in gold and silver. This, along with an enormous cache of grain, was intended to sustain them on the journey they intended to take with Christ to Jerusalem and pay for the rebuilding of the temple there. These riches were considered enormous in the 1800s.

As a communistic society, all needs of the members were met by the society, without money changing hands. Among other ventures, the town included a tailor, milliner (hatmaker), and cobbler (shoemaker). These merchants observed their fellow Harmonists at Sunday worship services. If they noticed a society member's clothing or shoes looking worn, they provided replacements free of charge.

Unlike many wilderness settlements, Old Economy Village had its own physician, Dr. Muller, who also indulged an avid interest in natural science. His collection of unique plant specimens can still be viewed at the village.

Father Rapp was a genuinely kind man and was beloved in his community. Even animals seemed to sense his gentle nature. A wild elk in the area befriended Rapp and often came and ate from his hand. Upon the elk's death, its head was mounted and now hangs in the museum.

Visitors to the town were impressed by the health and prosperity of the town and its inhabitants. The village was orderly, clean, and well managed. Most homes had family sheds. Many families trained their cows to come to the sheds to be milked, so that they did not have to find their cows in the common pastures. In addition, each home had its own garden plot, used for growing vegetables, herbs, and flowers.

In time, the death of George Rapp, coupled with the celibacy of the members, caused the success of the village to wane. By the late 1800s, few Harmonists remained. In 1905, the assets of the society were sold, and the land was purchased by the American Bridge Company, which renamed the town Ambridge. In 1916, the commonwealth of Pennsylvania acquired six acres of the original Harmonist land, along with seventeen buildings, with the intent of preserving them.

The Town Today

Today Old Economy Village is owned and managed by the Pennsylvania Historical and Museum Commission as a national historic landmark site and is open for touring. Admission is charged. A guided tour of six of the original buildings is clearly marked. In addition, you are encouraged to take a self-guided walking tour of Ambridge, which now encompasses what was formerly Old Economy Village. In all, 80 of the original 119 Harmonist family homes remain in the historic district of Ambridge.

A tour of the Baker House gives you an idea of how the Harmonists lived. The homes of George and Frederick Rapp stand nearby. Rapp's impressive garden, one of the earliest in the United States, has been restored. It was intended to replicate the Garden of Eden, including apple trees. A pavilion containing a beautiful statue of a woman with a lyre, surrounded by a pond, symbolizes a "woman clothed with the sun" from Revelations. Intersecting paths in the garden were meant to symbolize a cross. Grapevines growing in the garden signified the Last Supper, and the southwest corner of the garden represented the wilderness.

The Rapp home is beautifully furnished with well-made furnishings and fine wallpapers. This is somewhat at odds with Rapp's communistic beliefs, but it is theorized that because he was expected to host dignitaries at times, it was important that he represent the village in an impressive way.

The Feast Hall was the communal kitchen for the village. It contains twelve original pots, or cauldrons, which were used to prepare food for the town. The building also is notable for its unique roof, which contained trapdoors that could be opened to allow steam to escape while cooking. The hall was also used for the village library and classrooms, celebrations for various religious events, and concerts by the village orchestra.

Other buildings that are open for visiting are the cabinet shop, clockmaker's shop, and lock shop. The Mechanics Building contains the tailor shop, shoe shop, and print shop, which has the oldest flatbed printing press in America in its original setting. It was last used in 1832.

A blacksmith shop and barrelmaker shop host demonstrations, using tools from the era of the Harmonists. The blacksmith shop is not original and was built around 1900.

Directions

From the Pennsylvania Turnpike, get off at Cranberry, Exit 28. Follow Route 19 south to I-79 south and get off at Emsworth/Sewickley, Exit 66. Proceed to Route 65 north and follow for about 9 miles. Turn right at the Merchant Street stoplight. Turn left at the stop sign, go one block to 16th Street, and turn right. The Old Economy Village parking lot will be on your left.

COUCH'S FORT

A Revolutionary War–era defensive structure on the American frontier, Couch's Fort, in Allegheny County, saw more than its share of tragedy and drama as the expansion of white settlers in America spread farther and farther west.

History

Couch's Fort was built in 1788 on a tract of land consisting of more than 300 acres, located nine miles south of present-day Pittsburgh. Nathaniel Couch paid just over £3, British currency, for the property. Today that would translate to approximately $9. The fort was intended to provide some defense and protection from Indian attacks for the settlers along the frontier in Pennsylvania.

The Whiskey Rebellion in 1794 brought Couch's Fort some fame, albeit of a dubious nature. In an effort to generate money to pay back the debts incurred by the waging of the Revolutionary War, Alexander Hamilton, the new secretary of state, put forth a bold proposal. He urged Congress to invoke a tax on all distilled alcohol.

The money generated from the sale of whiskey was an important source of income for the farmers living on the western frontier in Pennsylvania. Bulk grain was difficult and costly to transport through the wilderness of the state. Instead, the farmers distilled the grain into whiskey, which was cheaper and easier to carry to market.

Despite this wise economic strategy of the farmers, the income earned from whiskey sales simply allowed them to continue to subsist on the frontier. The farmers were not enjoying great wealth from the transportation of liquor, but were earning just enough to remain living on the outskirts of the burgeoning nation. The new 9-cent-per-gallon tax presented a distinct threat to their livelihood and well-being. In addition, the farmers learned that the tax imposed on larger distilleries was only 6 cents per gallon. This seemed patently unfair.

The outraged farmers began to organize along the frontier and conduct raids on local tax collectors. Some of the hapless tax collectors were tarred and feathered, and others watched as their homes were set ablaze. The American government watched the developments in Pennsylvania warily and considered how to quell the disturbances.

It was during this time that Couch's Fort gained some notoriety. Frequently, the antitax rebels met at the fort to plan their activities. The meetings were raucous affairs, with plenty of alcohol flowing to fuel the men's passions. At the fort, the men planned to attack General Neville, the chief tax collector. More than 500 men descended upon Neville's home, assaulting him and burning the house to the ground. After the raid, the rebels returned to Couch's Fort to celebrate. The party lasted until well into the night.

The escalating uprising concerned George Washington, as it bore a disturbing resemblance to the Colonial uprisings that had launched the Revolutionary War several years earlier. He had no intention of facing his own people in war in the same manner that the British had not long before. He endeavored to crush the uprising before it gained more momentum.

The recently ratified Constitution of the United States gave Washington the right to mobilize a militia to quell the uprising, which he did, leading a force of 13,000 soldiers into western Pennsylvania. The military made a great show of power and potential force, but only halfhearted efforts to try to catch the rebels. The force was essentially unable to locate many of the protestors, although a few token arrests were made. The uprising ended. The tax was not collected.

The farmers soon moved their distilling operations outside the current country's boundaries, into what later became Kentucky, beyond the reach of the government. The unenforced tax was repealed in 1803.

The Whiskey Rebellion marked the first time that the American government exercised its right to take up arms against its own people.

The Fort Today

The original fort was torn down in 1890. In 1927, the Fort Couch Inn was built on the foundations. It was later renamed the Pioneer Inn, at which time the owners expanded and incorporated the chimney and fireplace into the structure. The Pioneer Inn was torn down to build a McDonald's fast-food restaurant in recent years. Aside from a historical marker, nothing remains of Couch's Fort today.

Directions

The site lies 9 miles south of Pittsburgh, in Bethel Park borough. The fort was located .6 mile south of the intersection of Fort Couch Road and U.S. Route 19, on the site of the current McDonald's.

ISELIN

Is Iselin truly a ghost town? Though it exists in a very different form today, it is still an inhabited community. As you stand in this Indiana County town, however, it is easy to imagine that you are in a bustling coal-mining town, as several of the original homes and buildings are still standing.

History

Iselin was founded in 1902, when Adrian Iselin's company bought 40,000 acres of land, which he spread among four separate businesses that he owned. He did this to circumvent an antitrust state law dictating that any one coal company could not own more than 10,000 acres in Pennsylvania.

Adrian Iselin was a banker in New York and a principal investor in the Rochester and Pittsburgh Coal and Iron Company. He was a very accomplished man, including being one of the incorporators of the Museum of Natural History and the Society for the Prevention of Cruelty to Animals (SPCA). He was a generous philanthropist to these organizations and died with a remaining fortune estimated at $30 million in 1905.

By May 1903, 400 workers had arrived to lay the foundations for the railroad, town, and mines at Iselin. By June 1904, the number had grown to 675. Many of the workers were immigrants from Italy, the Czechoslovakian region, and Poland.

A shanty town of huts and tents grew along the developing rail line. An entrepreneurial baker set up a huge outdoor oven nearby, supplying more than 1,000 loaves a day of fresh-baked bread to the workers and residents of the community.

Early Iselin was a raucous place. Living conditions were difficult at best. Bathing and other matters of personal hygiene were difficult to accomplish. Cold, wet weather made life in the tents miserable, with frozen toes and fingers becoming simply a normal part of life. Not surprisingly, entertainment and diversions were sought in any form. To meet this need, bootleggers supplied alcohol to the workers, which led to frequent brawls and riots.

Many of the men who built the railroad stayed on to become coal miners. By early 1904, a true town had begun to form. A hotel was constructed, which was a three-story wood building with thirty-nine rooms. It cost $9,000 to build, which was considered to be a fortune at that time. In addition, the town enjoyed a theater, school, train station, and company store. The inhabitants of Iselin worshipped at two churches in town, Holy Cross Roman Catholic Church and a Protestant church. The town was a busy, industrious place to live.

Some former residents recall how crowded the town was. Although there were more than 200 houses in Iselin, well over 1,000 residents crammed in. Houses could not be built fast enough to house the newcomers. Most families took in multiple boarders to meet this need, as well as to make a little extra money. Often the homeowners took in more boarders than there were beds. In such cases, after one man climbed out of bed to go to work in the mines, another returning from his shift would crawl into the warm bed to sleep. In the boarding-houses, the workers typically divided the cost of groceries and kept a close eye on what was purchased. They often tied distinctive strings to cuts of meat to claim them as their own and to make sure they got their share when the meal was served.

Like all coal mines, those at Iselin were dangerous job sites. Many workers were killed or injured extracting the ore from the five large mines that dotted the landscape. Most of the deaths were caused by falling slate, as mine safety at the turn of the twentieth century was quite poor compared with modern standards. Some deaths were also caused by runaway trains or mining cars.

Disease also was of great concern in Iselin, as it was in all corners of the world. The dearth of sanitation and overcrowding increased the threat. In 1911, a typhoid outbreak killed four citizens and sickened many more. Tainted water was the suspected culprit. Concurrently, a second mysterious disease spread through town, killing twelve, but this one did not appear to be contagious. The illness was traced back to ham and pork infected with cholera.

Social stratification within Iselin was notable. In the early days of the town, English-speaking inhabitants held themselves above those speaking foreign languages. This made for an uneasy alliance among Scottish, Irish, American, and Native American laborers. English-speaking workers often became foremen or other management-level employees. Europeans who did not speak English were given more menial positions, which caused dissension in the town. An obvious indicator of the division between cultures was the fact that the goal of many residents of Iselin was a home on English Street, a sign that one had "made it."

Two of Iselin's more celebrated townspeople, Dominick and Jack Ritchey, had emigrated from Venice, Italy. Gifted at masonry, they provided strong foundations for many of the homes in Iselin, as well as the mine drifts. Their work was sought after, as it was not only solid and well made, but also aesthetically pleasing.

Jack specialized in cement work. One of his more significant creations was the lovely railings on the porch of the Holy Cross Catholic

Church. Dominick specialized in painting ceiling frescoes, and some ceilings in what remains of Iselin still have traces of his paintings.

The beautiful cement markers in the Iselin Cemetery commemorating the Miners' Memorial are perhaps the greatest artistic legacy of the Ritchey brothers. Although somewhat degraded now, the memorial was beautiful when originally built, incorporating a miner's cap, carbide lamp, and shovel on the stone.

After World War I, as the demand for coal in America dwindled, families slowly left Iselin in search of financial stability. The mines closed for good in 1935.

The Town Today

Iselin still exists today, albeit in a very different form. Although it is now a suburban community, many of the original miners' homes still stand and are inhabited. The doctor's office remains and is a tile-constructed building with a hipped roof, one that is low-pitched to allow rain and snow to run off easily. The mine office, now a private residence, is a brick structure built on a stone foundation, also with a hipped roof. The town's fire hall is actually the original company store. There is a vacant lot where the Iselin Hotel stood. The churches are well used today, except that the Catholic church is now a busy day-care center.

The original Iselin mine complex is located south of modern-day Iselin, in Harper's Run Valley. The mine portal is intact, although the railroad, buildings, and actual mine workings are gone, obliterated by modern strip mining.

Directions

From Indiana, Pennsylvania, go west on Church Street. Turn left onto Oakland Avenue, Route 286 west. Follow for 14.5 miles, and turn right onto Iselin Road. Iselin is 1.8 miles north.

DILLOW'S FORT

Dillow's Fort, in Allegheny County, was an important site for the settlers of the area west of Pittsburgh. When word of imminent Indian attacks was heard, the settlers dropped what they were doing and raced for the safety of the fort.

History

After applying for a deed in 1778 for 400 acres and building a fort there, Michael Dillow was murdered by warring Indians while working in a field with his son. The younger man was captured but escaped after several years in captivity. After he made his way home, he retrieved his father's skeletal remains from where he saw him fall, allowing Michael Dillow to have a proper burial.

Despite the death of the fort's builder, the local settlers continued to use it for refuge from attack. Although the fort wasn't manned by a militia, it did provide some physical safety and a satisfactory defensive position for the local farmers and their families. But despite the fort's presence, some settlers still met with horrible fates.

In July 1779, William Anderson, a neighbor, was attacked by Indians and struggled to reach Thomas Armor's cabin, two miles distant from the fort. Armor carried Anderson the entire distance to the safety of the fort on his back, saving his life. When Anderson's wife had heard the ruckus, she grabbed her baby and hid in the woods, leaving behind her two sons, ages four and seven, who were playing near the cabin. The Indians found and captured the boys but were unable to find Mrs. Anderson or her baby. The two boys were never seen again.

The Fort Today

At one point a one-room school, called the Dillow School, was built on the foundations of the fort. Old lumber lying in the area is believed to be from the schoolhouse. Nothing remains of the original fort.

Directions

From Pittsburgh, take Parkway west to Route 22/30 west. Proceed 7.1 miles to a Y in the road, and bear left onto the Clinton-Frankfort Road. Follow this road for 3.8 miles, and turn left on Haul Road. After .6 mile, take a left on Dillow Road and go .2 mile. The fort was located on a shelf on the right side of the road, about a third of the way up the hill. If you look carefully, you can see tracks from Dillow Road to the site, on a diagonal path up the hill.

RICE'S FORT

The site of some bloody skirmishes, Rice's Fort, in Washington County, once served as a defensive structure on the American frontier.

History

Rice's Fort was built in the mid-1700s near Dutch Fork Lake. In its time, it was a well-known fort that provided significant safety and defense for the nearby settlers.

Indian attacks in the area were vicious and devastating. The worst raid occurred on September 14–15, 1782, when seventy Wyandot Indians attacked while most of the settler men were away trading. Several children and teenagers were killed as they tried to reach the safety of the fort. The six remaining men inside the fort successfully kept the murderous Indians from breaching the walls, thanks in part to the accuracy of their superb Pennsylvania rifles.

Abraham Rice, the owner of the fort, was returning from a trip when he heard the battle raging at his fort in the distance. He made a heroic attempt to ride straight through the Indians, which proved to be an almost suicidal move. He was shot in the arm and leg before retreating and escaping to nearby Lamb's Fort. The men of Lamb's Fort rallied, but they were unable to rout the Indians and returned to their own fort. The next day, the warriors gave up the attack on Rice's Fort and slipped away into the woods. The Lamb's Fort men gave chase but were unable to locate the Indians.

The Wyandots were not finished with their task of murdering settlers, however. As they left the area, they killed four more settlers a short distance from the fort.

Nearly a decade later, a single war party of Wyandots killed three men in one day on September 9, 1791: William Huston as he tended his corn, Jesse Cochran two hours later, and Benjamin Roger later in the day as he farmed. The following day, the Wyandots chased William Ayres, who ran for the safety of the fort but was murdered just before reaching it.

The Fort Today

The fort consisted of three blockhouses, which were connected to one another. A spring just to the west supplied water to the fort. The spring still exists today. The fort site is .1 mile beyond the small bridge on the right. Rice's Fort stood where the field behind a two-story brick house is today. The exact location was on the level portion of the field near the hillside. The land is privately owned by the owners of the brick house. Please check with them before entering the property.

Directions

To reach the site, take the Claysville exit off I-70 west. Turn right, then make the next left onto U.S. Route 40 west. Proceed 2.7 miles to Lake Road and turn right. Drive north on Lake Road for 3.2 miles. The fort site is .1 mile past the small bridge that is on the right.

WHISKEY RUN

A secret criminal society adds to the mystique of this colorfully named ghost town in Indiana County.

History

It is impossible to know for sure how Whiskey Run earned its name. One story tells of early settlers building a home on the site of the town, when they were approached by four drunk, belligerent Indians. The settlers feared for their lives but distracted the Indians from what they believed was an imminent attack by asking them to help split logs. As the inebriated Indians used their hands to pull at the wood on the opposite sides of a partially split log, the settlers struck. They knocked out the wedge holding the split apart in the log, trapping the Indians' hands inside. The farmers then murdered the Indians. Apparently proud of what they had done, the settlers named the site Whiskey Run, referring to the alcohol that the Indians had been drinking.

A somewhat less horrifying story states that the early Whiskey Run post office was actually running an illegal business selling untaxed alcohol. When word reached the post office employers that the tax men were on their way to the town, they poured their entire supply of liquor into the stream running through town.

The most likely reason for the name, however, is that bootleggers in town named it in honor of the creek that provided the necessary cold, clear water for their product.

However the town was named, it came into existence when the nearby town of Iselin found that the two coal mines it had dug to excavate the Elders Ridge Pittsburgh coal seam were inadequate to meet demand. The village of Whiskey Run was hastily built to house the workers at Iselin Mine #3. Many immigrants moved to the area for work in the mines.

Whiskey Run had a widespread reputation for lawlessness and violence. In 1907, a local newspaper reported on a pistol duel in the town, and the legend was born. Even though no one was killed in the duel, people for miles around began to steer clear of the rough streets of Whiskey Run. Did its name and reputation prove to be a self-fulfilling prophecy?

After the duel, many of the residents chose sides between the two men involved. The animosity between the two factions grew until violence again broke out. Brawls occurred frequently between these factions, until no one could even remember the reason for the initial fight. Once when mine managers accidentally assigned men from the two warring groups to a single train car, a gunfight broke out. One man was shot in the neck and another in the belly. The injured men had to be taken to separate hospitals in Indiana County because their friends continued brawling and rioting at the hospital, disrupting the other patients.

The living conditions in Whiskey Run undoubtedly contributed to the ongoing violence. Given the speed at which the town was erected, there were relatively few houses, which forced a dozen or so miners at a time to live in a single house with a host family, who charged the men for room and board. With so many men living under a roof with one or two women, problems were bound to occur. Jealous rages frequently led to violent fistfights or even murder.

In 1910, Moiden Nune, a Whiskey Run miner, was shot in the back, paralyzing him from the waist down. In the hospital, Nune swore that his landlady, a lovely young miner's wife, had shot him after he rebuffed her pleas for him to run away with her. Young Mrs. Mancanelli was arrested with her baby and imprisoned. Just before he died from complications from his wounds, Nune changed his story, admitting that Mrs. Mancanelli was innocent and he had instead been stalking her. She had shot him in self-defense. Mrs. Mancanelli was found innocent and returned to her husband in Whiskey Run. The town barely batted an eyelash at this drama.

Perhaps Whiskey Run's biggest claim to fame is that it was the site of the first quadruple homicide in Indiana County. Again, a young woman living in a home with multiple single male miners was the catalyst for the violence. Marie Bartino, a pretty teenager, was living with her family in Whiskey Run. As usual, the family had several boarders living with them. Apparently the majority of the men were in love with Miss Bartino. Three of the men began arguing one afternoon about who should have the right to court the young lady. The fight, not surprisingly, escalated into physical violence, with the three men rolling around, punching, kicking, and shouting. Into the mix came a fourth suitor, who arrived with flowers in hand, hoping to see Miss Bartino. He was quickly dragged into the melee. Miss Bartino watched in horror from around a door. The fistfight led to a gunfight, as at least two of the men had pistols. Three of the men died at the scene, and one lingered for several hours before expiring. Miss Bartino herself was struck by a bullet in the leg but survived.

A more sinister issue became apparent in Whiskey Run around 1920, when two men, Peter Villa and Camel Cosma, were shot and killed there. Police soon learned that Cosma had previously been injured in a mining accident and was receiving compensation. During his "recuperation," he had been traveling from his new home in Johnstown back to Whiskey Run on each payday. They found that Cosma required that the residents contribute some of their pay to his organization, the legendary Black Hand, a precursor to the Mafia. The group's spokesmen had told the locals that if they chose not to contribute to the organization, the Black Hand would arrange to have some of the miners' relatives killed in their native Italy. It was widely believed that these threats were credible.

Although no one would talk and the case was never solved, police believed that Cosma and Villa were killed by locals who had tired of the extortion. Cosma was shot twenty-four times, and Villa nine times.

Over the next few years, an unheard-of twenty-one unsolved murders were committed in Whiskey Run. In each case, the locals refused to give any information to law enforcement.

The town was never able to shake the reputation of being a frightening, violent place. Even after the company built churches and schools in the village, most people from neighboring towns avoided visiting.

The town began emptying out in 1928, as the workers began moving away. The mine closed down in 1934. Many of the townspeople loaded their belongings on the train and moved to the Detroit, Michigan, area. The homes in Whiskey Run were dismantled, and the building materials were taken to be used elsewhere.

The Town Today

Little remains of Whiskey Run today. Some of the neighboring towns have barns and sheds that were made from the Whiskey Run homes.

Directions

From Indiana, Pennsylvania, take Route 286 west. Turn right on Route 56 west. In the town of West Lebanon, turn left on Blackleggs Road. Make a right on Whiskey Run Road. The town was located around the current site of the township sign for Whiskey Run Road. Locals say that some rough foundations remain. No standing structures survive.

WELL'S FORT

Well's Fort, in Washington County, was the site of a daring Indian raid and subsequent rescue operation.

History

Alexander Mayfield built one of the earliest gristmills in western Pennsylvania in the late 1700s. To protect it from marauding Indians, he constructed an adjacent fort shortly thereafter.

Although it was an unusual structure in the area, the gristmill at Well's Fort was valuable to the locals, providing much-needed flour, as well as employment. History notes that when preparing to engage the local Indians in battle, Gen. George Rogers Clark used the mill to supply his troops, giving him a significant advantage over previous campaigns.

The mill also supplied flour to many other frontier forts. The value of the mill was not lost on the owner and the locals, who beseeched the government to send troops to protect them and the mill from the onslaught of the local Indians. In a rare acquiescence to such a request, Gen. William Irvine sent soldiers to protect the fort and ensure the continued provision of flour to the area.

The threat from Indian attack was ever present for the settlers. On March 27, 1789, a small band of Indians attacked the Glass family while the father was working in the fields. Mrs. Glass, her two sons, the family's slave woman, and the slave's young boy were captured. As they fled the ransacked cabin, the Indians murdered the slave child and left his body where he fell. The remaining captives continued on with their vicious captors, certain that their own death was only moments away.

When Mr. Glass returned home to the horror, he raced to Well's Fort for help. A heroic band of ten men trailed the Indians, who crossed the Ohio River with their captives before setting up camp. The Indians relaxed, believing that the river had obliterated all trace of their location.

Fortunately, one of the Glass boys had dropped a piece of white paper on the ground at the place where the war party crossed the river, enabling the settlers to follow the trail across the river. The rescuers stormed the Indians' campsite, wounding the Indians, who fled into the forest. The remaining captives were rescued, unharmed.

The Fort Today

A white house now stands on the spot where the fort once stood.

Directions

The site of Well's Fort is in the center of Avella, just a few miles east of the state line to Ohio. Follow Route 50 west from Pittsburgh. At the point where Route 50 ends at a T intersection, the fort stood where the center of the T is.

WEHRUM

Wehrum is a ghost town in several senses of the term. Although it was a successful mining town for a time, this Indiana County community was also the scene of great tragedy. Was it also a cursed town?

History

The town of Wehrum was founded in 1909. It was named for Henry Wehrum, who was the general manager of the Lackawanna Iron and Steel Company at the time. The town was built around an enormous coal-mining operation owned by the Lackawanna Coal and Coke Factory (a subsidiary of the Lackawanna Iron and Steel Company), based in Scranton.

In 1903, the Pennsylvania Railroad extended service through Wehrum, providing a way to transport coal from the mines. It also allowed for increased passenger train service, which brought larger numbers of people to Wehrum.

Lackawanna Mine #4 opened as a shaft mine in 1902. It had a capacity of producing up to 2,000 tons of coal per day, an impressive amount. The coal mined was washed in the enormous coal washer in Wehrum, and then transported by train to Buffalo, New York, for use in making coke in the Lackawanna Steel Plant located there.

At its busiest, Wehrum boasted almost 250 houses, two churches, a school, post office, hotel, bank, and company store. The town was laid out on a grid of six streets, each of which was sixty feet wide.

From almost the beginning, Wehrum seemed to be living under a dark cloud. What had all the makings of an incredibly successful coal operation was fraught with problems, and it never truly reached its potential.

In 1904, four coal miners were killed when methane gas exploded in the mines. Following the catastrophe, the mining continued, but only on a part-time basis, two to three days per week. In August 1906, the coal washer burned to the ground. Although it was rebuilt in 1907, its initial loss had a devastating effect on the amount of coal being brought out of the ground. The raw coal being brought out of the mines was considered to be too dirty to use in steelmaking, rendering the mines almost useless until the washer was rebuilt.

By 1908, the coal mining had tapered off alarmingly. In December, it was calculated that only 61,000 tons of coal had been produced that year.

At 7:40 A.M. on June 23, 1909, the town of Wehrum awakened to tragedy. A gas explosion in Mine #4 killed twenty-one and injured twelve others. By 7:30 that evening, the grieving families had recovered their loved ones. In a town of 300 families, the loss of so many of their own was shocking.

The accident devastated the town. Although limited mining continued, a slow decline had begun. In 1922, the mines and associated buildings were sold to Bethlehem Mines Corporation. The new company did little to increase the mining operations in Wehrum, and the mining families began to move away from the area. The houses were dismantled, the boards and foundations carted away to other towns. By 1934, the only structures left in Wehrum were one house, the jail, the school, and the Russian Orthodox Cemetery.

On July 19, 1977, the Wehrum Dam collapsed, one of six that contributed to the horrific flooding of Johnstown. It seemed a fitting ending to a town that had traveled on a path of sadness throughout its brief history.

The Town Today

Little remains today of the town of Wehrum. What does remain reportedly stands on private lands, so you need to get permission before exploring. The site lies along the Ghost Town Rails to Trails, which runs from Nanty Glo to Dilltown. Wehrum is well marked from the trail.

Eerily, one of the only remaining vestiges of Wehrum is the cemetery, which was formerly a part of the Sts. Peter and Paul Russian Orthodox Church. Most of the graves in the cemetery are those of children.

Directions

Take the Pennsylvania Turnpike to the U.S. Route 220 exit toward Bedford/Altoona/Johnstown, and take U.S. Route 220/I-99 north. Get off at the U.S. Route 32 exit (Exit 28) toward Ebensburg/Hollidaysburg. Merge onto Route 22 west, also known as the William Penn Highway. Travel just over 32 miles and make a right onto Wehrum Road. Stay right and follow the road for a little over 2 miles. There is a parking area in Wehrum for the Rails to Trails Ghost Town Trail. A seasonal bathroom facility is also available. From the trail, the site of Wehrum is easily found, as a sign marks its location.

South-Central Pennsylvania

PANDAMONIA

The ghost town of Pandamonia, in Perry County, is slowly disappearing into the Tuscarora State Forest, but it is not forgotten. Someone continues to place flowers on the graves of the long-gone inhabitants of "the abode of all demons."

History

Pandamonia was a relatively long-lived town, lasting from 1797 to 1912. One of its earliest inhabitants was Christian Henry, for whom Henry's Valley was named. Around 1840, I. J. McFarland purchased a large parcel of land in Henry's Valley, near Pandamonia, and built a large steam tannery. The tannery building was located on the north side of Laurel Run, downhill from the town.

The town grew to include two sawmills, a barrel stave factory, and a store. At its height, as many as 100 homes dotted the mountain.

The name Pandamonia is reported to mean the abode of all demons. The story of how the town earned its name is the subject of some dispute, as no written records of it remain. Legend tells of a tumultuous argument among the townspeople over the language in which religious services should be practiced. After a long, loud struggle between the German and American members of the town, one man supposedly shouted, "We may as well name the town Pandemonium, because that is what this is."

Pandamonia was an isolated enclave of strong individuals. There was little luxury or entertainment to be found in the town. To visit a store for anything other than the staple products carried here, residents had to walk or ride a horse more than eight miles to Landisburg or Newville. In addition, the valley did not have telephone or postal service, so the townspeople had to travel the sixteen-mile round-trip for these basics as well.

Henry's Valley School was located just south of the town cemetery. The school building also functioned as a part-time church on Sundays for the townspeople. It was built shortly before the start of the Civil War.

One particularly poignant story has been passed down through the generations at Pandamonia. It is unclear whether it is true, as no written record can be found. The legend tells of a young black girl who escaped slavery in the South by way of the Underground Railroad. She made it as far as Pandamonia, traveling by night. Upon reaching Pandamonia, some of the local dogs chased her, barking loudly. The girl climbed a tree to escape the dogs, which continued snapping and lunging at her from below. Some of the townspeople were roused from their beds by the din. In the thick darkness, they mistook the girl for a treed bear and shot her from the tree, killing her. The townspeople were mortified and heartbroken. The young woman is reportedly buried in the Pioneer Cemetery in an unmarked grave, near the white oak tree in the northeast corner of the graveyard.

The tannery changed hands several times over the years and finally closed in the late 1800s. When the tannery folded, the residents of Pandamonia began to move away from the area. Farming proved to be too difficult in the rocky soil of the valley, and no other industries replaced the lumber businesses. By 1912, the area was essentially deserted.

The Town Today

The most obvious remnant of Pandamonia is the Pioneer Cemetery, which continues to be well tended today. Plastic flowers decorate the graves, and flags adorn not only the two Civil War veterans' graves, but also the fence surrounding the cemetery. It is well marked for visitors, with a clearly visible sign on Laurel Run Road.

About seventy-five yards south, down the hill from the cemetery, is the site of the Henry's Valley School. It is also well marked with a sign on Laurel Run Road. The foundations of the school are somewhat visible, mostly lingering in piles of rocks. Scattered in the forest around the school site and the cemetery are more incongruous piles of rocks, suggesting possible sites of past homes. Gazing at these apparent home sites, it is easy to imagine how comparatively populous Pandamonia must have been.

South of the Henry's Valley School, .2 mile down Meadow Road, are the sites of the steam tannery and sawmills, again well marked with signs. The foundations suggest several very large structures just north of what is now Laurel Creek. Remains of one of the steam pipes lie just east of the foundations. When visiting the tannery site, wear sturdy, water-resistant boots, as the area is rather boggy, with numerous springs bubbling to the surface around the foundations.

Directions

Take Route 233 from Landisburg, in Perry County. Turn right on Laurel Run Road, shortly past the Sheaffer Valley Church. Laurel Run Road is a forest road, which is a dirt road in good condition. Most vehicles should have no difficulty reaching Pandamonia. Travel approximately 5 miles, until you see the sign for Henry's Valley School on the right, not far past the sign designating a Civilian Conservation Corps (CCC) site from the 1930s.

GREENWOOD FURNACE

Greenwood Furnace is now a lovely state park in Huntington County, with some preserved buildings that serve as reminders of a time when the iron industry in Pennsylvania was a thriving, lucrative business.

History

In the 1700s, white settlers arrived in the midstate area. Because of the endless lush forests, the area became known as Greenwood. A small village by that name sat nestled in the valley near what would later become State College. Settlers maintained homes and a tavern in the area until the actual town of Greenwood Furnace was established in 1834 by Norris, Rawle, and Company. The town's furnace began smelting iron in June of that year. At its height, it put out more than 1,200 tons of pig iron ingots per year.

Greenwood Furnace was unique in that it had two operating stacks, placed side by side. The stack on the left was fueled by a water wheel, and the one on the right was powered by steam. The second stack was built to meet the increasing demand for iron from the Freedom Iron Works. Making the furnace more valuable, in 1839 a large vein of high-quality iron was found nearby.

Col. John A. Wright purchased the iron furnace and the Freedom Iron Works from Norris, Rawle, and Company in 1847. Two years earlier, Wright had been a founder of the town of Altoona, as well as the Pennsylvania Railroad, which was based there.

To provide fuel for the furnaces, men called colliers made charcoal. From April through October, the colliers worked hard, limiting the amount of air the burning wood received. The men stacked thirty-five to fifty cords of wood onto hearths and covered them with underbrush and dirt. They then lit the piles with fire and tended the smoldering flames constantly. After a couple weeks, the wood had burned down to charcoal. One batch of charcoal fueled the furnace for a day and a half.

The colliers were a hardy lot. They took pride in their blackened appearance. Cleanliness was seen as a sign of inexperience. As a result, their huts were consumed by charcoal dust, which invaded the beds, the floors, the walls, and certainly the lungs of the worker. Because they rarely bathed, all manner of vermin and filth were a part of life for the colliers. Their smell announced them long before they strode into view. Their employers were not naive about their living conditions: At the end of each season, the colliers' huts were torched, to be rebuilt in the spring.

Workers from Greenwood Furnace transported the iron by wagon from the furnace to the Freedom Iron Works, where it was turned into wrought iron. The wrought iron, in turn, served to outfit the burgeoning railroad industry by providing the axles and wheels for the railroad cars.

A town quickly grew around the furnace. A mansion was built for the ironmaster. A company store met the material needs of the community and also served as an informal meeting place for town residents. Ninety houses provided shelter for the 300 employees and their families. The community also supported seventeen stables, a blacksmith shop, gristmill, baseball team, and brass band. In 1842, the community built a recreational lake next to the gristmill in order to provide power to the mill.

As the world turned its attention to alternative fuels and materials, Greenwood Furnace declined in demand and output. The older stack was retired in the early 1880s. The second stack was remodeled and enlarged, but these efforts were not enough to prevent the business from total failure. The second furnace poured its last ingot on December 7, 1904. The Greenwood Furnace residents gathered around as the company's steam whistle sadly blew for the last time.

The residents quickly relocated, and all remaining businesses folded. The town was largely dismantled. The commonwealth of Pennsylvania purchased the ironworks lands in an effort to reforest the damaged timber stores of the area. The charcoal ash released by the ironmaking process had served to enrich the local soil, making the area ideal for reforestation. The Greenwood Furnace Tree Nursery existed from 1906 until 1993. During the 1970s and 1980s, the land produced 3 million tree seedlings per year.

The Town Today

Although the nursery operations are no longer in effect, the state still owns the land, which now functions as a picturesque state park that is open to the public. Several buildings from the furnace era remain standing and are available for tour at Greenwood Furnace State Park. Stop at the clearly marked ranger station for information and maps of the walking trail.

The furnace stacks still stand in good condition. The blacksmith and wagon shop nearby now hosts the visitors center. A wagon in front of the building was used at Greenwood Furnace to haul iron to the Freedom Iron Works. The buildings that housed the meat house and company store also remain. They have been preserved to appear the way they might have in the mid-1800s.

Near the lake, which is open to the public for swimming in summer, lie the foundations of the gristmill. Across Route 305 from the lake is the cemetery, which has twenty-seven marked and forty unmarked graves. The cemetery came into use in 1850 and ceased being open to burials in 1926. It contains the remains of two Revolutionary War and six Civil War veterans.

The Methodist Episcopal church is a lovely one-room structure that continues to provide religious services in summer. It was built around 1865 and is a popular site for weddings today. Across the road from the church is the Ironmaster's Mansion, a three-story home with fourteen rooms built in 1833. It has been well preserved and can be toured.

The Bookkeeper's House, built in 1863, stands today. Although initially bookkeepers lived in the Ironmaster's Mansion, as the importance of the bookkeeper to the business became more evident, grander living quarters were deemed appropriate. The Bookkeeper's House is a private residence and is not available to tour. It should be viewed only from the road.

Directions

To reach Greenwood Furnace, follow Route 26 south from State College. Turn east on Route 305. Greenwood Furnace State Park is located on Route 305 at the intersection with Broad Mountain Road. It is clearly marked. The park is a 35-minute drive southeast of State College.

FORT ROBERDEAU

Fort Roberdeau, in Blair County, was commanded by a brave and successful American hero.

History

Fort Roberdeau was a Revolutionary War–era fort constructed in 1778 by Gen. Daniel Roberdeau to protect a mining operation from the frequent Indian attacks in the area. The American government had become aware of a vein of valuable lead that ran through the Sinking Spring Valley. It was critical that the patriots not only mine the lead, but also prevent it from falling into enemy British hands.

During the war, the demand for lead was intense. The metal was used to manufacture bullets, an absolutely crucial commodity during the war. Lead had been found on a 9,000-acre tract in the Sinking Valley, prompting the state of Pennsylvania to seize the land and begin mining operations. Plans for the fort, also known as the Lead-Mines Fort, were hastily made. The fort's construction was problematic, however, as the topsoil in the area was very shallow. But with some clever engineering, construction was completed by early 1779.

The fort's defenses were provided by the Bedford County Militia, led by Cap. Robert Cluggage. The fort provided refuge for local settlers when Indians attacked, although no accounts exist of the fort itself being attacked.

Daniel Roberdeau was an accomplished man even before founding the fort in Sinking Spring Valley. He was the first person elected to the rank of general in the United States, promoted to the position on July 4, 1776, by the Associators of Pennsylvania. A precursor to today's National Guard, the Associators were a group of patriots organized in a system of state divisions devised by Benjamin Franklin.

Roberdeau was a wealthy businessman from Philadelphia, renowned for his love of freedom and all that the burgeoning United States stood for. He was elected as a representative for Pennsylvania to the Second Continental Congress. He also served as a member of the Procurement Committee for the army, responsible for making sure that the troops had what they needed to effectively wage war. In addition, he served on the Intelligence Committee, which strove to learn what strategies the enemy was employing to attack the patriots.

When the Intelligence Committee learned of the lead deposits in the Sinking Spring Valley, General Roberdeau volunteered to verify the report and secure the ore. He took a leave from Congress in 1778 to make his way to the valley. He stopped in Carlisle en route to requisition troops and supplies for the fort and arrived in Sinking Spring Valley in April.

At the time of Roberdeau's arrival, many residents of the area were leaving because of raids by the local Iroquois Indians, as well as the threat of attack by British soldiers. General Roberdeau strove to reassure the locals that the fort would protect them. He also reminded them of their duty to remain on the edge of the frontier and not to relinquish it to the enemy.

General Roberdeau's bravery extended beyond his willingness to protect the American frontier. Later in life, Roberdeau visited England. While traveling by carriage in the countryside there, he was set upon by highwaymen intent on robbing him. Roberdeau grabbed the leader of the gang and dragged him into the carriage. He then shouted to the driver to drive on. As they raced away from the scene, Roberdeau fired his pistols at the highwaymen, who fled. The coach made its way to London, the lead robber's feet still protruding from its window. Roberdeau ordered the driver to make his way directly to the magistrate, where the thief was handed over to face justice.

The mining operations at Fort Roberdeau were a failure. There are two theories as to why this is so. One argument states that the cost to mine and smelt the ore into usable lead exceeded the profit that could be made. In addition, the amount of lead that lay within the earth had been exaggerated. Others believe that the British Loyalists in the area threatened and bribed the miners to stop mining. Roberdeau, in a final attempt to make the mine a success, offered the miners bonuses of $100 to finish smelting the ore that was already mined, but they turned it down. This theory holds that although the British never did attack the fort physically, they successfully shut down the lead production nevertheless.

After the mining operations ended, the troops left Fort Roberdeau abandoned. It continued to be used as an unmanned refuge for the local residents for some time but eventually fell into disrepair.

The Fort Today

By the 1940s, interest in restoring the fort began to build. At that point, the only portions remaining were the walls of the powder magazine and some stonework of what was believed to be the smelting forge. On July 5, 1976, the Blair County Restoration Committee dedicated the fort as a Bicentennial Project.

Blair County now owns the land that the fort once occupied and has worked hard to restore it as an educational and historic site. The Fort Roberdeau Historic Site and Natural Area consists of 230 acres in Sinking Valley and is open from May 1 to October 31. The restored fort is available to tour. In addition, a visitors center and museum shop are housed nearby in a restored barn from around 1858. There are picnic facilities and nature trails for hiking. An admission fee is charged. Reenactments are held periodically throughout the year, during which local reenactors create an eighteenth-century military field camp on the grounds of Fort Roberdeau.

Directions

From Altoona, take Route 220 to Kettle Road and turn north. Continue on Kettle Road for about 8 miles to Fort Roberdeau, which is well marked.

Southeastern Pennsylvania

EASTERN STATE PENITENTIARY

Does Eastern State Penitentiary qualify as a ghost town? Inhabited, it covered more than eleven square acres within Philadelphia and housed hundreds of tormented souls. Many would argue that it houses a number of those souls even today.

History

In the late 1700s, there was a growing tide of concern about the conditions of the nation's prisons and the living conditions of the prisoners kept within. This was especially true in Pennsylvania, the home of the Quakers. A Quaker group called the Philadelphia Society for Alleviating the Miseries of Public Prisons approached Benjamin Franklin with their belief that the current state of prisons in America w deplorable. The society's goal was to devise a new system for appro ing incarceration: implementing a penitentiary.

Before the concept of a penitentiary, prisons were horrific places, with the main goals being punishment of the prisoners and keeping them from continuing to victimize society. In both Europe and America, many prisons kept men, women, and at times even children in the same large holding cell. Those who were awaiting trial were kept in the same area as criminals who had committed horrendous crimes.

Prisoners victimized one another with impunity. Conditions were of the roughest sort: Beds were minimal or nonexistent, there was no heating system or toilets, and some prisons did not provide food. A prisoner's relative comfort was often heavily reliant on his or her ability to pay cash to the jailer. The money could be used for food, bedding, liquor, release from shackles, or even the ability to come and go from the jail at will. Wealthier prisoners were even allowed to bring prostitutes with them into the prison. Prisoners without money were often forced to sell articles of clothing to buy food for survival and slept on the cold, filthy floor of the holding pen. Prisoners who could not pay the jailer for their meals often had to reach their hands through the bars to the street outside, begging passersby for their food.

Another concern was "jail fever," probably typhoid fever or something similar, which spread unchecked among the inmates and was often fatal. Jailers, visitors, and even jury members risked contracting the disease.

The Philadelphia Society for Alleviating the Miseries of Public Prisons proposed an entirely new way of approaching incarceration. They wanted to build a prison that was designed to induce true regret in the criminal, causing the prisoner to reflect on his or her crime and do penance for it. Thus the concept of a penitentiary was born.

The concept was considered radical, and it took more than thirty years for the idea to become palatable to the legislature of the commonwealth. Finally it was decided that a penitentiary would be built on a large plot of farmland near Philadelphia.

Eastern State Penitentiary, originally named Cherry Hill, officially opened in 1829. The building and its grounds were massive, and at the time it was the most expensive American structure ever built, costing $772,600. It soon became famous internationally for its progressive model of incarceration. Illustrious visitors, including Charles Dickens, made their way to view this new model of dealing with criminals. Not all were impressed with what they saw. Dickens, for example, saw the methods employed at Eastern State as dehumanizing and created to drive the prisoners insane.

The Quakers, who initially spearheaded the campaign to use penitence as a way to make prison a more productive form of punishment, believed that isolation and silence were the keys to forcing prisoners to reflect on the horror of their crimes. Minimizing distractions and sensory input facilitated the prisoners' likelihood of ruminating on their misdeeds.

When prisoners entered the penitentiary, they were hooded so as to minimize the amount of the prison that they viewed. They were assigned numbers and were not referred to by name again until they were released from prison. Talking was not permitted at all in the penitentiary, neither to other inmates nor to guards. Each prisoner was led to a cell measuring eight by twelve feet, which would be home for the duration of the incarceration. For twenty-three hours a day, the prisoner sat alone in this cell, seeing only the occasional guard, who did not speak to him or her. One hour per day of exercise was permitted in a small yard next to the cell. Prisoners in adjacent yards could not go out at the same time. The only book available to the prisoner was the Bible. No other diversions were allowed.

No visitors were permitted throughout the period of incarceration. The only person allowed to speak with the prisoners was the overseer, who periodically stopped by to offer counseling or training in a trade. The prisoners were not permitted to hear news of the outside world, including who the current president of the United States was.

Despite a goal of improving living conditions, Eastern State's cells were rather uncomfortable. They tended to be musty and stale, and dampness often leached in through the walls and floor. There was little air circulation, and coupled with the faulty sewage system, it made for a foul-smelling institution. The architect had devised a central heating system for the penitentiary, but it worked rather poorly. Prisoners were allowed to bathe only once every three weeks, and the smell of unwashed bodies added to the already fetid air of Eastern State.

At times the prisoners attempted to contact one another. This was strictly forbidden. Prisoners who were caught tapping on bars to communicate with another, whistling, singing, or talking to themselves were punished with lost meals or put in a blackened, empty cell for several days.

The silence in the penitentiary was profound. The guards did not speak and wore socks over their shoes to mute the sound of footfalls. In doing so, they were also able to spy on the inmates and easily catch any infractions. Paranoia among the prisoners was rampant and well founded. They never knew when the guards were peeking in through the peepholes and might catch them quietly talking to themselves or whistling songs. Either infraction would be met with a few days in blackness in the isolation chamber, a place feared by all.

Occasionally more serious violations of the rules occurred. Punishments for these more severe infractions included loss of a sleeping blanket in cold weather or being chained to a cell wall. A "shower bath" was used at times by some of the more sadistic guards. This strategy consisted of chaining a prisoner wearing only pants to a wall outside in winter and then pouring cold water on the culprit. At times, it was cold enough for ice to form on the prisoner's skin.

But the harshest punishment dealt out at Eastern State was the use of the "iron gag," a five-inch piece of metal, somewhat resembling a horse bit, that was placed over the prisoner's tongue. The guards then handcuffed the prisoner with the hands behind the back, pulling the hands up until they were almost behind the neck and chaining the iron gag to the handcuffs. Therefore, if the prisoner fought the gag or pulled at all with the arms, the gag would dig deeper and deeper into the mouth. Moving the arms at all could cause severe damage to the prisoner's mouth, so the arms had to remain in the awkward, painful position until released. One prisoner reportedly died from the use of this device. Almost all prisoners subjected to this punishment suffered terrible pain and damage to their mouths.

Mental illness, not surprisingly, was a constant issue at Eastern State, although the management of the penitentiary downplayed its prevalence. The isolation, the sensory deprivation, the punishments, the uncomfortable living conditions, and the loss of many things that make one a human being drove many prisoners to madness.

The guards suffered in their own ways. The silence in the prison, along with the boredom of making the rounds, led many to drink alcohol while on the job. Indeed, at one point the guards were given a daily ration of liquor during the day in an attempt to prevent them from overindulging. This strategy failed, and the guards drank even more. Eventually the prison commission cracked down and fired anyone found drinking on the job.

It wasn't all unpleasant at Eastern State Penitentiary, however. The prison prided itself on providing superior medical care to the inmates. In addition, the food was far superior to that served in other prisons. The penitentiary was relatively clean and safe. "Jail fever" was almost unknown at Eastern State, although the foul conditions from the sewage issues created other health problems.

The Quakers believed that productive work was one of the keys to true penance, so the prisoners were expected to work in their cells. They made shoes, wove fabric, or produced other goods. If prisoners did not know a suitable trade, they were taught and required to perform one.

By the mid-1900s, prison crowding throughout the commonwealth forced jailers to make changes to Eastern State Penitentiary. The concept of isolation and silence was abandoned as multiple prisoners were assigned to cells. The hoods and iron gags were disposed of, and Eastern State began to resemble many other overcrowded prisons.

Eastern State housed some colorful characters. One of the more illustrious prisoners was Al Capone, who was imprisoned there for eight months in 1929. He spent his time at the penitentiary in relative luxury, enjoying a cell with lovely artwork, a radio, and a beautiful wooden desk.

Another well-known resident of Eastern State was the bank robber Willie Sutton. He and eleven other men made news when they tunneled out of the prison in 1945. Although prisoners digging tunnels was not rare here, Sutton's tunnel was unique in that it had fans, lights, and structural supports. Unfortunately for the prisoners, all of the escapees were recaptured shortly after reaching the end of their tunnel on Fairmount Street.

The Penitentiary Today

Eastern State was closed in 1971. Although it had been designated as a national historic landmark, there was talk of turning the site into a shopping mall or even high-rent condominiums.

Instead, the prison was kept as a monument to a well-intentioned experiment in incarceration. It still stands much as it did when it was built and has become one of Philadelphia's most popular tourist attractions. Peeling walls, dark corridors, and an overwhelming sense of foreboding greet the many tourists who visit the penitentiary annually. The prison was used as the setting for the movie 12 Monkeys, starring Brad Pitt. Guided tours are available from April through December. Group tours, if arranged ahead of time, can be done in winter as well.

Halloween is a busy time for Eastern State Penitentiary. The prison has gained a reputation as being haunted, and many high-profile paranormal groups have investigated it, often with intriguing findings. The penitentiary has capitalized on this interest, providing several excellent ghost tours during the fall season.

People have reported seeing shadowy figures darting among the cells, accompanied by a drop in temperature and great feelings of dread. Others say they saw a ghostly figure standing in one of the guard towers. Cell Block 12 is generally regarded to be one of the more active paranormally. Visitors sometimes claim they heard the sounds of laughter emanating from some of the cells.

One of the more disturbing encounters has been recounted by many visitors and employees of the penitentiary. A shadowy, dark, human-shaped figure stands perfectly still, often unnoticed, until a visitor ventures too close. At that point, the shape dashes away. This figure was presumably caught on film recently by a televised paranormal group.

Whether one believes in the paranormal or not, Eastern State Penitentiary is a foreboding, fascinating place to visit.

Directions

Take I-76 (the Schuylkill Expressway) to Exit 344. This is I-676, also known as the Vine Street Expressway. Take the first exit, the Benjamin Franklin Parkway/23rd Street exit. Turn left onto 22nd Street. Pass the Philadelphia Museum of Art and continue north for five more blocks. The penitentiary is located on Fairmount Avenue.

EPHRATA CLOISTER

A devout religious community once inhabited a picturesque village in Lancaster County.

History

In 1730, a group of German immigrants formed a new Protestant religious group, the German Seventh Day Baptists. They lived in an area of Lancaster County along the Cocalico River, named Ephrata. One of the goals of the sect was to embody William Penn's dream of religious tolerance and integration.

The members devoted their lives to drawing closer to God, eschewing material wealth and worldly pursuits. Their leader, Conrad Beissel, was a former baker from the Palatinate region of Germany. During his formative years, Beissel had become involved in the growing religious dissension in southwestern Germany. He and his fellow dissenters were displeased with the established religions in their land. Beissel wanted to seek a closer, personal relationship with God, as opposed to having an intermediary, such as a priest or pastor, speak to his God for him. Beissel appreciated the idea of mysticism, the belief that one's relationship with God was more important than that which could be provided by a member of the clergy.

Beissel was also inspired by the Pietism movement, which put forth the concept that the worshipper's personal and spiritual relationship with God was more important than rote recitation of creeds and liturgy. Instead of having formal church services, Pietists met informally in groups to share ideas and support one another.

As Beissel became more and more immersed in his radical beliefs, he began to deny the validity of the established churches in Germany. His refusal to attend services and his expression of dissenting opinions caused him to be expelled from the Palatinate region in 1718.

Beissel was not alone, however. Almost a million emigrants left the Palatinate region in the 1700s. Many went elsewhere in Europe, but some made their way to the American colonies. Most of the immigrants in America sought out the colony founded by William Penn, who was a Quaker. The Quakers' beliefs were similar in many ways to Beissel's. Penn, in return, welcomed them, recognizing their ability to contribute agriculturally and economically to the burgeoning commonwealth of Pennsylvania.

Beissel eventually began preaching in the Conestoga region of Pennsylvania, later known as the Lancaster area. He taught that one must turn one's back on material pursuits, and that the relationship with God must be a marriage, with complete devotion and attention. Because of this belief in marriage with God, Beissel called for his faithful to be celibate. In order to meet the needs for full attention and spiritual connection with the Creator, humans should separate themselves, to some degree, from the secular world.

Following his beliefs, in 1732 Beissel left his flock to live as a hermit in a hut on the banks of the Cocalico River. He looked forward to spending his days alone, seeking spiritual fulfillment and closeness with God. His followers had other ideas for him, however. They came to the settlement and asked him to continue to provide spiritual guidance. A small village of huts soon was built around Beissel's cabin.

By 1735, it was obvious to Beissel that a more structured organization was needed for his congregation. He began the construction of a dormitory and named the burgeoning village Ephrata, which translates from biblical language to mean "suffering." The dormitory, named Kedar, contained both celibate men and women. It also provided space for solitary prayer, working, and dining.

There were some married people in Beissel's order, who were referred to as Householders. They did not live in the dormitory, but in other lodging in areas just outside the village.

Word spread of Beissel's community, and soon other German-descent immigrants began arriving. Building at Ephrata continued at a rapid pace to meet the demand. The community was roughly triangular, which pleased the mystic in Beissel, who viewed the triangle as a perfect shape.

The buildings at Ephrata resembled structures from the residents' native Germany. The rooflines were more steeply pitched than other Pennsylvania homes of that era. Clay-lined fireplaces heated the buildings and doubled as cooking ovens. The buildings were rather spare and utilitarian, without luxuries or many material possessions. Beds were hard and uncomfortable, having no mattress or pillow.

Ephrata was an austere place. In keeping with the belief that the residents existed solely to draw closer to God, laughing, gossiping, or being lighthearted was frowned upon. Instead, followers were urged to be quiet and meditative, keeping camaraderie and conversation to a minimum.

The Ephrata members all dressed similarly. The men, or Brothers, wore monastic-appearing robes with pointed hoods. The Sisters' robes were similar but had rounded hoods instead. Few of the sect members wore shoes, although they were permitted. Instead, they went barefoot, even in cold weather.

There were many religious occasions at Ephrata, but one of the most important was the Love Feast, a three-part ceremony that often lasted several hours in duration. The first step was that of washing the feet of one another. This was reminiscent of Christ washing Magdalene's feet, as well as a washing away of one's sins. The second part of the ceremony was the meal, which often included meat, a luxury that was rare at Ephrata. The final step was the presentation of bread and wine for communion. Beissel enjoyed presiding over the communion himself.

Besides the Love Feasts, which were held frequently but not on a particular set schedule, the sect members rose every night at midnight for religious services. The midnight services were generally two hours in duration. Even in bitter cold weather, the faithful rose from their beds and made their way to the chapels to worship. Following the service, the members returned to bed, only to reawaken at 5 A.M. to begin their workday. They generally worked for nine hours, with four one-hour breaks built into the day for meditation and prayer. Two hours were set aside each evening for formal spiritual study, and one hour was designated for dining.

Beissel obtained a rare printing press on which he published many documents. The Ephrata Cloister became regarded as a rather important source of publication. The sect printed on paper produced at its own paper mill, using its own manufactured ink. Members tanned the leather for the covers in their own tannery.

One of the best-known products to come from the Ephrata Cloister was Fraktur, a folk-art form that many Germans in America practiced, creating documents such as birth certificates and marriage announcements. The Ephrata Cloister members drew intricate ornamentations in the Fraktur tradition on delicate paper produced at their own mill.

Ephrata began to decline when a sect elder named Israel Eckerlin proposed capitalizing on the commercial advantages of the paper mill. Many Ephrata members, including Beissel, opposed this, believing that the materialism that would result from commercializing the community's resources would undermine the spiritual underpinnings of the group. Eckerlin eventually left to form his own Ephrata but was captured by the French during the French and Indian War. On being freed in 1764, he returned to Beissel's Ephrata, causing some dissension in the community, which viewed him as a catalyst for opposition and turmoil.

Conrad Beissel's death in 1768 caused a crisis in Ephrata. The community was briefly without leadership, and fears that the sect would disband spread throughout the village. Into the gap, Peter Miller reluctantly stepped. He had performed the duties as Beissel's second in command for some time and knew that a void in leadership would end the community. Miller believed that the community would not survive much longer anyway, despite leadership, as the American society was changing. Independence from Britain was imminent, and the dreams of success in a free America were difficult to ignore. Other communistic societies had found the lure of material wealth too powerful to resist.

After Peter Miller died in 1796, the community slowly dissipated. By 1813, when the last two celibates died, the fate of Ephrata Cloister appeared to be sealed. Some of the Householders were astute enough to preserve the traditions that Beissel had begun and to value what Ephrata had stood for. Although some of the assets, including the printing press, land, and mills, had been sold, a core of Ephrata remained until 1943, when the congregation was formally dissolved. The Pennsylvania Historical and Museum Commission acquired the property and set about restoring and preserving it.

The Village Today

Thanks to extensive preservation and restoration efforts, several of the original Ephrata Cloister buildings still stand today and are open for touring. Some of the buildings remaining include Beissel's House, the Saal (meetinghouse), Saron (the Sisters' house), a weaver's house, carpenter's house, printing office, and bakery. God's Acre, a cemetery, is also on-site and includes the graves of Conrad Beissel and Peter Miller.

Orientation materials are available at the visitors center. An admission fee is charged to tour the site. Many artifacts are available to view in the buildings and give you a sense of what life must have been like for the sect members.

Directions

From Lancaster, take Route 222 north to the Ephrata exit, at Route 322 west. Turn left off the exit and proceed on Main Street for 2.5 miles. The entrance to the Ephrata Cloister is on the left side of Main Street and is clearly marked.

RAUSCH GAP

Located a short drive from the state capital, Rausch Gap, in Lebanon County, is a treasure trove for ghost town enthusiasts.

History

Rausch Gap began as a town sometime around 1828. The coal mine was founded by a Dr. Kugler, who planned to exploit an anthracite vein that ran through Sharp Mountain. Kugler also had business interests in the Daupin and Susquehanna Railroad. After mining operations began, it became obvious that railroad service was essential to move the coal from the rugged slopes of Sharp Mountain, and the Dauphin and Susquehanna built a hub in Rausch Gap.

Rausch Gap became a center of railroad activity. The town grew in size and population, and it peaked at about 1,000 residents. The townspeople found employment at both the coal mines and the railroad.

By 1851, Rausch Gap contained more than twenty homes and several other buildings. At least fourteen homes were clustered near the machine shop, which reportedly was 160 feet long. The homes in Rausch Gap were company houses, provided to the workers as furnished dwellings with central fireplaces for warmth. The men were paid 50 cents a day in wages, but most of their earnings went directly to room and board. In fact, to live in one of the nicer homes in town, workers paid their entire salary for room and board, with nothing left over.

Rausch Gap apparently experienced some social stratification. Shanties scattered in the woods around the main area of Rausch Gap reportedly belonged to Irish immigrant workers, who were considered to be of a lower class than other employees.

The mines and railroad employed mostly adult male employees. In the days before child labor laws were enacted, however, it was common to see small boys hard at work beside the men. The children were held to the same productivity standard as their adult counterparts and were often physically punished when they did not perform.

A tragic train accident occurred just outside of Rausch Gap. A young man named Mason English had been fishing with friends near Clarks Valley. Having no luck catching fish, he decided to hike to the Rausch Gap area to do some hunting for groundhogs. In the heat of midday, Mason decided to lie down to nap. He chose to nap on the railroad tracks, as the creosote covering the railroad ties acted as a mosquito repellent. He covered himself with hemlock branches to further discourage the buzzing insects.

The Dauphin and Susquehanna train came along right on schedule. The conductor saw a pile of branches on the track but did not realize that a person lay beneath them. Mason was hit and killed, with his head severed from his body, as well as other horrific injuries. To compound the tragedy, he was carrying his brother's fishing license, so he was identified incorrectly for some time, causing great distress to his family members. The story made headlines in every newspaper in the area.

Although some mining continued into the 1930s, the majority of the anthracite mines were closed in the 1870s when the supply of coal ran low. In addition, the railroad headquarters were moved to the town of Pine Grove, in Schuylkill County. With most employment gone, the town rapidly declined. Rausch Gap was a ghost town by 1910, and most buildings were torn down.

The Town Today

Hikers on the Appalachian Trail pass right by Rausch Gap, which is clearly marked with signs. Many foundations remain, scattered around the area. You can also see remnants of homes, the machine shop, railroad turntable, and the coal breaker. Wander around the area a bit, as many foundations are not depicted on the map sign provided.

Down a separate, clearly marked trail is a small cemetery. Only three graves have standing headstones, although it is believed that there are many more unmarked graves in the plot. One grave is that of John Proud of Durham, England, a worker who died in his fifties. The stone reads: "Affliction sore long time I bore; All human skill was vain; Till God did please to give me ease; And free me from my pain."

To heap another hurt on this poor soul, vandals dug up the grave in the 1970s and flung the remains around the area. What little was found was reinterred, but the grave lies essentially empty. Other graves include that of Andrew Allen, who died in a mining accident in nearby Gold Mine in June 1854, and Catherine Blackwood, a baby who died two weeks after Allen.

The railroad turntable remains are across the creek from the town, near the scenic trestle bridge. Although only foundations are visible, it is easy to imagine the trains being turned on the structure. The coal breaker was located some distance away, just south of where the Appalachian Trail clubs have built an outhouse. As you hike toward a Rails to Trails path from the outhouse, you can see the remains of the enormous coal breaker as stone foundations terracing the steep hillside.

Directions

Rausch Gap is easy to find on any Appalachian Trail map. If you choose to drive in, it is a simple four-mile hike from the parking area.

Take I-81 to the exit for Lickdale/Lebanon, Route 72 (Exit 90). Turn left onto Fisher Avenue, and then turn left onto Route 72 north. After Route 72 passes through Swatara State Park, it will become Route 443 east. Continue on Route 443 to Gold Mine Road on the left. Turn left and follow Gold Mine Road to the top of Second Mountain, and then descend into the valley where the Stony Valley Rail-Trail crosses the road. There will be a state game lands sign on the left, with a small lane leading to a parking area. Park there and begin hiking on the gated Rails to Trails path.

The sign for Rausch Gap is 4 miles down the trail and is clearly marked. To find the shanty foundations, railroad turntable, and coal breaker, some off-trail searching is required. In spring and summer, many foundations may be obscured by vegetation. Use caution while exploring, as the wells used by the townspeople are still present in the area and are not always clearly visible.

FRICKS LOCKS

Skulking in the shadows of the PECO Nuclear Energy Plant in Chester County is the largely intact ghost town of Fricks Locks.

History

The town of Fricks Locks was founded sometime around 1815. It was named for the original landowner, John Frick, who sold the land to the Schuylkill Navigation Company. A series of locks was constructed on the adjacent Schuylkill Canal to improve barge commerce in the area. The locks enabled the barges to be slowly raised or lowered with the level of the river, without having to traverse rapids or other dangerous obstacles.

In the 1980s, it was determined that the newly built power plant towering over the town posed a significant health risk to its inhabitants. The residents of Fricks Locks were paid for their homes, and all moved away. It has stood empty ever since.

The Town Today

Fricks Locks is in remarkably good shape. About ten intact buildings still stand along the single road winding through the village. Among them, Frick Mansion, the Lock Keeper's House, and the general store remain in relatively good condition. There are also several outbuildings, such as barns, summer kitchens, and storage sheds.

The houses, though officially boarded up, have open doors or windows in at least one location, making entrance easy. Be extremely cautious when exploring this town. The village has a very isolated feel. In many homes, there is evidence of people vandalizing or partying. No evidence of squatters was seen, but I strongly advise against exploring the town alone.

Besides the threat from one's fellow man, the more immediate threat is from structural instability and other hazards in the houses themselves. The older homes in the village are relatively sound, structurally, but you must take great care when exploring. No electric lights exist, so darkened stairways, hallways, and rooms make encountering hazards likely. In many of the structures, the integrity of the rooftops has been compromised, and rainwater has soaked the floors repeatedly, putting them at risk of collapse.

Several of the more recently built homes near the entrance gate are completely unsafe to enter. The roofs and multiple floors have fallen in, sometimes even into the cellars. Use extreme caution and sense when exploring. Carry a flashlight, wear sturdy closed-toe shoes and work gloves to protect from splinters, and have a cell phone for emergencies.

Directions

From Reading, take Route 422 past Pottstown to Route 724, and head toward Phoenixville. In just under 1 mile, you will see the sign for Fricks Locks Road on the left. Follow it to the yellow gate closing the village's road. Park near the gate and proceed on foot into the village.

COLD SPRINGS RESORT

With ladies carrying parasols and loving couples strolling down the promenade, Cold Springs Resort lent a touch of class for a time to the outer reaches of Lebanon County.

History

You can almost hear the faint whisper of a string quartet floating through the trees as you approach the former Cold Springs Resort. It is easy to imagine ladies wearing bustles and carrying parasols strolling with dapper gentlemen past the foundations of what was once a glamorous resort hotel complex. If you listen closely enough, maybe you can hear happy campers laughing . . . or perhaps the shout of a drowning soldier.

The story of Cold Springs, like many ghost towns, is one of lost dreams and great disappointments. Over the history of the land, many of its owners dreamed of making a viable luxury resort, capitalizing on the supposed therapeutic qualities of its water. But over and over again, such ventures failed.

At its most successful, the Cold Springs Resort boasted two beautiful hotels, side by side. They were stunning three-story Greek Revival buildings. Formal columns punctuated the views from the porches and balconies. A shady lane served as a promenade for ladies in long, elegant dresses and gentlemen with top hats and canes.

Visitors partook of the therapeutic springs in the main bathhouse, which had several plunge baths as well as showers. It is believed that the bathhouse had stained-glass skylights, rather than wall windows, to protect the modesty of the bathers within. The mineral water in the springs may have had some therapeutic effects, but vacationers attempting to bathe in it were in for a breathtaking shock from the 48-degree temperature of the springs. Graffiti from the period on the bathhouse walls states that only the strongest of men could withstand the temperature for more than two minutes.

Dancing often took place during the evening in a large converted barn. In addition, the resort boasted lawn tennis, croquet, a billiard room, and a rare feature—a bowling alley. Those preferring slightly warmer waters could swim in the local lake, called Lake Dresden until World War I, when German names fell out of favor. It was later rechristened Lake Comey.

Although the resort initially was popular during summer months, a succession of owners had great difficulty maintaining financial solvency. Few guests were interested in visiting in colder weather, and the resort often stood mostly empty.

The advent of the Civil War caused one of several declines in the history of Cold Springs. Economic hardship made expensive vacation travel to such a resort unrealistic. In 1864, Israel Brandt became the caretaker of the deteriorating resort. He and his family catered to an increasingly seedy group of boarders. By the time Brandt's wife died of tuberculosis in 1867, he began to find himself being drawn into the criminal circles that occupied the hotel's rooms.

In 1878, Brandt, along with three other men, met an insurance agent at the hotel. They told the agent that they would like to insure

Brandt's elderly neighbor, Joseph Raber, for $8,000. In return, they promised to care for Raber throughout his life. Raber, a poor man who lived in a charcoal burner's hut in the mountains near the resort, cooperated with the transaction, which named the four younger men as the beneficiaries.

Later that same year, the four conspirators hired two men to drown Raber in Indiantown Creek. Although the death was initially deemed accidental, the son-in-law of one of the conspirators came forward as an eyewitness to the murder.

The six men were dubbed the Blue-Eyed Six because of the coincidence that they all shared the same eye color. The story was reported worldwide. On April 24, 1879, after only five hours of deliberation, the jury returned a guilty verdict for first-degree murder for all six of the accused. The Blue-Eyed Six trial apparently was the first trial in the United States in which conspirators were held as responsible as those who had actually performed the murder. On appeal, one of the conspirators was acquitted for lack of evidence. The other five were sentenced to death by hanging and were executed.

Besides the legal precedent of finding conspirators equally guilty as murderers, the case was also noteworthy because it dramatically changed insurance law in the United States. Following the verdict, massive changes made it much more difficult to insure someone in whom one has no legal interest.

Raber was laid to rest in the cemetery of the Moonshine Church nearby. Although paranormal enthusiasts continue to flock to the cemetery under the mistaken notion that the Blue-Eyed Six are buried there, research indicates that the conspirators were buried elsewhere throughout the state. Nevertheless, persistent rumors of hauntings in the churchyard, including seeing six sets of blue eyes glowing in the dark, continue to this day.

The resort's popularity suffered even further following Brandt's arrest. The association of the conspirators with the elegant hotel made travel there unfashionable.

The resort finally came to a dramatic and apocalyptic end in September 1900. Following an unsuccessful attempt to sell the property at a public sale, the current owner, Henry Moyer of Lebanon, was finally rid of the responsibility when it burned to the ground. Shortly after the last summer visitor had left, the resort mysteriously caught fire, and most structures were completely consumed by the flames. Although rumors circulated that Moyer had started the blaze to collect on the insurance, nothing was proven.

After the resort burned down, an attempt was made to capitalize on selling the mineral water by starting a bottling company on the site. But like most other ventures at Cold Springs, this one too was short-lived.

In the early 1920s, the YMCA of Camden, New Jersey, purchased the tract and opened the Shand Boys' Camp. The price of the property was $2,010, the extra $10 for a mule that came with the property. Boys came to camp on the rail line, which had resumed service following the devastating fire. Improvements totaling more than $40,000 were made to the property, including repairing some structures and constructing new ones. The bowling alley, which had escaped the fire, was converted into housing units.

Around 1940, a tragedy occurred at Cold Springs. Several soldiers from Camp Edward Martin (now known as Fort Indiantown Gap) hiked onto the property, carrying a large amount of beer in their backpacks. After apparently becoming drunk, they decided to take some of the camp's canoes, minus oars, for a spin around the lake. A soldier fell into the water in the deepest part of the lake and drowned. His body was found near the camp's diving platform by the waterfront director of the camp, after he was alerted to the incident by the surviving soldiers. The sad incident cast a pall over the camp, and talk circulated about closing it to further use.

As the United States became involved in World War II, the boys' camp was permanently closed. Counselors had found recent artillery shells embedded in the trees surrounding the campers' tent area. The shells had come from nearby Fort Indiantown Gap. The discovery was sufficiently alarming to warrant disuse of the camp.

The story of the Cold Springs Resort is ultimately a tale of lost hope and failure. Time and time again, enthusiastic entrepreneurs had attempted to capitalize on the natural beauty, the mineral water, the rail line, or the interest of vacationers, only to have the property sink back into poverty and desertion. Despite the wild beauty of the land, as you look at the crumbling foundations of the hotels, the lake where the soldier drowned, or the cemetery at the Moonshine Church, you may begin to question how so much disappointment and tragedy came to be concentrated on one tract of land.

The Site Today

There are a great many foundations, steps, and ruins at the Cold Springs site. The foundations of the two hotels are still very visible and in decent condition. The foundation of the caretaker's cabin and the ruins of the bowling alley stand nearby. Stone foundations where the still-flowing springs once hosted stalwart souls in their frigid waters remain, as do the supports of the water tank, which is located just uphill from the hotel site. The land and the ruins of the resort now belong to the State Game Commission, although current disputes over land rights may give Fort Indiantown Gap ownership of the land as a firing range.

Directions

From Interstate 81 in Lebanon County, take the Fort Indiantown Gap exit and drive to the Gap. Take Route 443 northeast past the Gap until you see signs for Hawk Watch. Follow the signs for Hawk Watch to the left until you meet the intersection of Cold Springs Road. This is a rather rugged road in places. Unless you have a four-wheel-drive vehicle, it is recommended that you park in the lot at the top of the mountain. If you are brave, there is a parking lot at the bottom of the mountain, not far from the Cold Springs site. This lot overlooks a large field that was the site of Camp Shand.

BIBLIOGRAPHY

Books and Articles

"Alvira: Village Is Just a Memory Now." *Milton Standard,* October 8, 1987.

Aurand, Harold. *Coalcracker Culture: Work and Values in Pennsylvania Anthracite, 1835–1935.* Selinsgrove, PA: Susquehanna University Press, 2003.

Bernard, Lou. "The Potential Location of Fort Reed." Clinton County Historical Society Document, Lock Haven, PA, 2006.

Biles, John. *Historical Sketches Pertaining to or Linked with Asylum.* Geneva, NY: W. F. Humphrey Press, 1931.

Blatz, Perry. *Eckley Miners' Village: Pennsylvania Trail of History Guide.* Mechanicsburg, PA: Stackpole Books, 2003.

Bradley, John. *Ephrata Cloister: Pennsylvania Trail of History Guide.* Mechanicsburg, PA: Stackpole Books, 2000.

———. "Pushing William Penn's 'Holy Experiment' to Its Limits: The Ephrata Cloister." *Pennsylvania Heritage Magazine* 22, no. 4 (Fall 1996): 14–23.

Buckalew, John. "The Frontier Forts within the North and West Branches of the Susquehanna River." Published in the *Report of the Commission to Locate the Site of the Frontier Forts of Pennsylvania,* 1896.

Casler, Walter. *Tionesta Valley.* Self-published, 1973.

Clarke, Stanley. "The Laquin Lumber Company." *The Settler: A Quarterly Magazine of History and Biography* 25, no. 1. (1928): 32–33.

Cooper, Eileen. "The Iselin Family Left Its Mark on the Pennsylvania Coal Fields." Special Collections, IUP Libraries, Indiana, PA, 1981.

Darah, William Culp. *Pithole: The Vanished City.* Self-published, 1972.

DeKok, David. "Government Was Slow in Helping Residents." *Patriot News,* May 27, 2002.

————. *Unseen Danger: A Tragedy of People, Government, and the Centralia Mine Fire*. New York: IUniverse.com, 2001.

Eggert, Gerald. *The Iron Industry in Pennsylvania*. Pennsylvania Historical Association, 1994.

"The Federal Government Broke Its Promise." *Milton Standard*, October 8, 1987.

Gates, Nancy. "Dream Town." *Central PA Magazine* 20, no. 2 (August 2000): 10.

Johnson, Deryl. *Images of America: Centralia*. Charleston, SC: Arcadia Publishing, 2004.

Johnston, Norman. *Eastern State Penitentiary: Crucible of Good Intentions*. Philadelphia: Philadelphia Museum of Art, 2000.

Kline, Benjamin. *"Stemwinders" in the Laurel Highlands*. Self-published, 1973.

————. *"Wild Catting" on the Mountain*. Self-published, 1970.

Lake, Matt. *Weird Pennsylvania*. New York: Sterling Publishing Company, 2005.

Logan, James C., and James M. Logan. *Cold Springs Hotel Site: Uncovering Its Layers of History*. Lebanon, PA: Lebanon County Historical Society, 2005.

Lontz, Mary Belle. *History of the Schools of Union County*. Self-published, 1984.

Murray, Elsie. *Azilum: French Refugee Colony of 1793*. Athens, PA: Tioga Point Museum, 1950.

Pettanati, Waldo. "Norwich Was a Bustling Little Town . . . Before It Vanished." *Bradford Era,* May 27, 1993.

Reynolds, Patrick. *Pennsylvania Profiles Series*. Willow Street, PA: Red Rose Studio, 1974.

Richards, John. *Images of America: Early Coal Mining in the Anthracite Region*. Charleston, SC: Arcadia Publishing, 2002.

Rickenbach, Joel. "The Historic Village of Fricks Lock." *Eerie, Pa. Magazine* 1, no. 1 (Fall 2006): 54–58.

Rupprecht, George. "Lost Teutonia: The Experimental McKean County German Communist Community." Unknown source.

Snyder, Charles. *Union County, Pa.: A Bicentennial History*. Lewisburg, PA: Colonial Printing House, 1976.

————. *Union County, Pa.: A Celebration of History*. Lewisburg, PA: Union County Historical Society, 2000.

Stephenson, Clarence. *Indiana County 175th Anniversary History*. Indiana, PA: A. G. Halldin Publishing Company, 1989.

Stiver, Wendy. "Little Town Has Intriguing Past, Quiet Present." *Lock Haven Express,* February 8, 1989.

Taber, Thomas. *Ghost Lumber Towns of Central Pennsylvania*. Self-published, 1970.

————. *Sawmills among the Derricks.* Self-published, 1975.

————. *Sunset along Susquehanna Waters.* Self-published, 1972.

————. *Tanbark, Alcohol, and Lumber.* Self-published, 1972.

————. *Whining Saws and Squealing Flanges.* Self-published, 1972.

Troy, Mabel. "Laquin." *The Settler: A Quarterly Magazine of History and Biography* 11, no. 8 (1952): 20–29.

"The Valley Lost Three of Its Churches." *Milton Standard,* October 8, 1987.

Watts, Brandy. "Rausch Gap History." Unpublished work, 2005.

Websites

http://cip/cornell.edu/Dienst/UI/1.0/Summarize/psu.ph/1133209646

http://famousamericans.net/danielroberdeau

http://hometown.aol.com/fricklocksvillage/myhomepage/profile.html

http://peale.bravehost.com

http://ccj.sagepub.com/cgi/content/abstract/18/4/394

http://womenshistory.about.com/library/etext/bl_nlmj11.htm

www.abandonedbutnotforgotten.com

www.bradfordhistory.com

www.cumberlink.com/articles/2006/10/29/news.news17b.txt

www.dcnr.state.pa.us/stateparks

www.eckleyminers.org

www.explorepahistory.com

www.fortroberdeau.org

www.frenchazilum.com

www.ghosttowns.com

www.greencracker.com/2003/08/the_town_of_pan

www.homestead.com

www.lib.iup.edu/spec_coll/articles/whiskey_run.html

www.logwell.com

www.mcintyrepa.com/Aiselin.htm

www.missioncreep.com/mw/estate.html

www.motherbedford.com

www.muzzleblasts.com

www.mysite.verizon.net/warholic/trail.html

www.mywebpages.comcast.net/StAnthonyWilderness/anthony.htm

www.ncpenn.com

www.northumberlandcountyhistoricalsociety.org

www.norway.org

www.questpublish.com/museumnet/

www.patheoldminer.rootsweb.com

www.phmc.state.pa.us

www.pottercountypa.net/history

www.prairieghosts.com/eastern.html

www.rootsweb.com/~pasulliv/settlers/settlers17/settlers17.html

www.rootsweb.com/~pasulliv/sullivancountyfolk/scf3/Ricketts.htm

www.shulersnet.com/coalcracker/history.htm

www.smethporthistory.org

www.trails.com

INDEX